MAKING SENSE OF CHILD SEXUAL EXPLOITATION

Exchange, abuse and young people

Sophie Hallett

D1610900

P

First published in Great Britain in 2017 by

Policy Press
University of Bristol
1-9 Old Park Hill
Bristol
BS2 8BB
UK
t: +44 (0)117 954 5940
pp-info@bristol.ac.uk
www.policypress.co.uk

North America office:
Policy Press
c/o The University of Chicago Press
1427 East 60th Street
Chicago, IL 60637, USA
t: +1 773 702 7700
f: +1 773-702-9756
sales@press.uchicago.edu
www.press.uchicago.edu

© Policy Press 2017

British Library Cataloguing in Publication Data
A catalogue record for this book is available from the British Library

Library of Congress Cataloging-in-Publication Data
A catalog record for this book has been requested

ISBN 978-1-4473-3360-9 paperback
ISBN 978-1-4473-3358-6 hardcover
ISBN 978-1-4473-3361-6 ePub
ISBN 978-1-4473-3362-3 Mobi
ISBN 978-1-4473-3359-3 ePdf

Cover design by Hayes Design
Front cover image: www.alamy.com
Printed and bound in Great Britain by Clays Ltd, St Ives plc
Policy Press uses environmentally responsible print partners

MIX
Paper from
responsible sources
FSC   FSC® C013604

For Martin 'Bart' Johnson

Contents

Acknowledgements

First and special thanks go to all those whose stories and accounts form the centre of this book. I am so grateful to all the young people who participated. Thank you for being so open and willing to share your thoughts, for giving your time and for your enthusiasm and support for the research. I hope that you felt and feel heard in having done so. To the professional participants too, I am so grateful to you for your generosity in giving your time and for sharing your thoughts and stories.

Thank you to Jan Coles and Sam Clutton for your interest and support in this work, and thank you also to all the practitioners at the voluntary service where much of this research took place. I am grateful to Health and Care Research Wales (formerly the National Institute of Social Care and Health Research), for the award which facilitated this research.

Many thanks to Professor Andy Pithouse for encouraging me to begin the research on which this book is based, and for being a fine supervisor for its duration. Special thanks also to Dr Tom Hall – previous supervisor, teacher, current mentor and great friend – for your continued and unfailing support and encouragement, intellectual influence and discussion. Both Tom and Andy have a claim over this book (if they wish to make it).

Heather Montgomery deserves a special mention for taking time out from her own significant commitments to read and comment on a final draft of this manuscript. Your thoughtful and constructive comments were invaluable and I am very grateful. Many thanks also to the three anonymous reviewers who commented on my proposal, and to the anonymous reviewer who gave helpful comments and feedback on the draft of this manuscript. Many thanks also to Helen Thomas for reading the first draft and checking it made sense to a 'lay' reader. Isobel Bainton at The Policy Press has been a supportive editor to work with and I offer her my sincere thanks.

There are a number of colleagues and friends I wish to thank. Special mention to the CASCADE team for bearing with me in the office, giving me space and for shared understanding. Thanks to Finn Bowring, for your helpful discussion and advice when developing the proposal for this book and for your encouragement in my final few days of writing. Thanks also to Ceryn Evans, Elaine Russ, Jenny Molyneux, Becky Booth, Jesse Smith, Dave Horton, Kirsty McQueen and Les Back, for your encouragement, and for the pleasure of shared interests in (and redirecting my attention to) music, literature and the occasional film.

Many thanks to my big and varied family, for feigning interest in a topic that most people avoid, and generally for having firmly instilled in me the gift and ability to laugh at myself. Family also includes Jen and Steve, who have also been hugely supportive. Finally, I am indebted to John, who deserves very special thanks for all the dog walking, cooking, not-minding, and general 'being there-ness'.

The close up is the opposite of a statistic.

(John Berger, 'Recognition')

Introduction

In 2009, 'child sexual exploitation' officially first entered UK social care policy and practice lexicon. Its introduction into public discourse has been slower, occurring mainly on the back of serious case reviews and high profile criminal trials in Rotherham, Rochdale, Oxford and Derby in 2013 and 2014 (see Jay, 2014; Ofsted, 2014). Around the same time, police Yewtree investigations into historical sexual abuse cases by those in power and with celebrity, symbolised by 'the Jimmy Savile case', meant that 'child sexual abuse' and 'child sexual exploitation' featured almost daily in UK national news reports. Concerns around young people's sexualised behaviours, the uses and abuses of social media and the risk of 'grooming' have also been raised. UK society has discovered what was unknown, and 'CSE', as it is most often referred, alongside its synonym 'grooming', is talked about as an emerging form of abuse: a new social problem.

Yet child sexual exploitation is not new. As I will outline, young people abused through the exchange of sex has a lengthy social history – indeed the past 100 years have seen it feature as a re-emerging subject of welfare policy, practice and public concern; and one resurfacing in various guises (see Brown and Barrett, 2002). Concerns and panics around young people's sexuality – when it is legitimate, when it is abused – are also not new (see Hebdige, 1988; also Phoenix and Oerton, 2005). I do not pass comment on whether we are in the throes of a new 'moral panic', as some have argued (see Cree et al, 2012); however, it is clear that, while it is not possible to know with reliability the scale of the problem, we can be sure that the harms experienced by the young people in these sorts of circumstance are significant.

But what is 'child sexual exploitation'? What makes it different to other forms of child sexual abuse and why has the terminology and the issue itself taken so long to appear in social care policy and public awareness and understanding? This book aims to provide an empirically and sociologically informed answer to these questions. At its heart are perspectives from two groups who are central to the issue: young people with experiences of sexual exploitation, who are the subject of much investigation and policy directed interventions; and professionals operating in various fields (such as healthcare, youth work, education, social care, policing, social work) and who play a key role in identifying and supporting young people who may be so involved. The book explores the ways these participants made sense of the problem of child sexual exploitation and what can and should be done about it.

In so doing, I take a critical perspective, and also address the possibility that (further) problems might arise from the way in which 'child sexual exploitation' is conceptualised. The book develops an analysis that is critical of a social and policy discourse that defines and provides an explanation for 'child sexual exploitation' according to a grooming model – in which children and young people figure predominantly as the passive victims of predatory adult perpetrators. 'Grooming' has become the way of both explaining and understanding how young people come to experience CSE. I argue that such a focus is narrow and narrowing, and can have an inhibiting effect in regard to grasping young people's actual experiences, silencing those whose experiences of sexual exploitation do not fit within this conception, which can limit what professionals see, label and act upon when faced with a young person in need, while also having serious implications for the ways that society responds to CSE and to the individual children and young people caught up in it. There are three core arguments made in the book, which revolve around the concepts youth, power, childhood and care. First, the book argues that intrinsic to CSE is the element of exchange, and underpinning this is the meeting (and exploitation) of unmet needs; second, conceptions of CSE may be problematic for *young people*, particularly with regards to understanding and framing young people's agency; third, 'care' (relationships, systems and acts), particularly in the context of power and recognition, sits at the crux of the problem of CSE.

Note on the language

'Child sexual exploitation' is more than just a neutral, descriptive policy term for a social problem that can be understood and addressed once labelled in this way; the term itself is caught up in a particular framing of the problem, one which I look to unpack throughout this book. Acronyms too do their part in framing the way that we see and understand the world, phenomena and people. Describing the subject of concern is by no means straightforward, yet we must call it *something* – hence the following conventions have been deployed. I apply the categories 'prostitution' and 'child sexual exploitation', or CSE, as a reference to historical or contemporary policy and practice discourse and my occasional use of single quotation marks is a necessary reminder to the reader that the terms are not being used uncritically. I sometimes adopt the less objectifying term 'sexually exploited', the more neutral phrase 'exchanging sex', or refer to 'the problem', as a means to convey a sense of distance from the narrow and sometimes distorting parameters of CSE as policy construct. However, when considering the participants' accounts I utilise and reflect back their own phrasing. This varied approach is unavoidably messy but provides the essential contrast and difference that facilitates nuance, insight and the layered analyses that are called forth by this complex phenomenon.

The research

The data, analysis and discussion considered here is based on my doctoral research. There are many ways that one might go about research. Observing practice is one way; large scale questionnaires, drawing on statistics or case file analysis are others. This research was designed as a qualitative case study inquiry, utilising participatory methods, semi-structured interviews, and a year-long fieldwork placement in a specialist CSE project working with children and young people.

The overarching aim was to provide an in-depth understanding of child sexual exploitation by exploring the understandings and perspectives of young people with experiences of it, and of professionals who hold key roles in identifying, referring and working with young people who may be so involved. My intention was twofold: I sought to provide practice and policy relevant insights into this social problem, while also seeking to provide a more discursive academic exploration into the social construction of this social issue. This particular approach is not meant to be 'representative' in terms of numbers of participants: the importance and significance of the findings come from the detail and layered richness of the data, so giving the *grounds to generalise* rather than quantitative generalisability (Arksey and Knight, 1999).

The research participants

As this book rests firmly on the accounts of those who participated in the research from which it draws, it is necessary to introduce them. Nine young people took part in this research. It is with some care that I use the term 'young people'. It is used as a descriptive category, and I assert that this is not a homogenous group of participants. While I acknowledge their diversity, there were commonalities that mark them as a 'research set', and it is perhaps helpful to situate the sociology of the participants here. The young people were aged between 14 and 17 years old at the time of the research. Eight were female and one male. All were white Welsh/British, and 'working class' by dint of parent occupation. All of the young people had experienced some involvement from Social Services in their lives. Eight of the young people were, or had been, 'Looked After Children' – the subject of care orders and placed in the care of a local authority (for two of them this was specifically related to concerns around their risk to sexual exploitation). These eight had experienced periods of living in residential and foster care, or of living with different family members for periods of time. All were in receipt of support from a specialist voluntary sector service, and all had been referred for reasons related to concerns about sexual exploitation. For ethical reasons, details about their particular circumstances and experiences related to their exposure to what is termed 'sexual exploitation' are not disclosed. Moreover, it is one of the purposes of this book to allow young people to speak for themselves, and it is in the next chapter that they do so. That said, it is necessary to provide some context, and as such Melrose (2012) gives a usefully broad definition to draw on: they each had experience(s) of the 'exchange of sex for some form of pecuniary reward or some form of material benefit' (Melrose, 2012: 159).

While their accounts are retrospective it is important to note that the young people were at different stages of emotional and temporal distance from the circumstances and relationships they talked about: indeed, some were not distant at all and were still engaged in abusive relationships and circumstances. Some had been removed from the situations they described (by being placed in foster or residential care away from their home area, or they were in secure accommodation). Some were being supported to remove themselves from troubling situations and to 'stay safe'. Others were in the process of being supported to ensure there would be no repeat of these experiences. Accordingly, none could be considered – or considered themselves – to have fully 'moved on' (if at all). The young people involved in this research were making sense of that which they were to some extent still involved in. Furthermore, they are young people who were being supported specifically for reasons related to sexual exploitation, by a number of different professionals. This is an important point in that these were young people who have been 'worked with' therapeutically, who had been spoken to and who had spoken about their experiences. Their framing of events in interview may therefore reflect something of the ways in which they had already disclosed and reflected upon CSE with care professionals; however, this does not 'devalue' their accounts or make what they have to say somehow 'inauthentic'.

The research also involved 25 'non specialist' professionals from across three local authority areas in South East Wales. They are referred to as 'non specialist' in that working in the field of child sexual exploitation is not a key part of their role; they represent the range of professions listed within the Wales (and other UK relevant) policy and practice guidance as holding key roles in the identification, referral and prevention of child sexual exploitation. They each held frontline positions, from within education; policing; youth justice; social work; youth work; community work; general practice and sexual health; third sector social care organisations; and fostering. Of the 25, 13 were male, 12 were female. Their professional experience of working with young people spanned from between eight months to 35 years. The three local authority areas chosen provided both an urban and rural context to the research and encompass the areas in which the young people lived. It is this which marks them out as being of particular interest as a research set. It was not the intention to make any kind of comparative analysis between these professionals. While I recognise the diversity of these participants in their background, occupation, and range and length of experience of work with young people, I nonetheless use the term 'professional' as an inclusive and homogeneous category for the purposes of this research.

Ethics and reflexivity

The research was informed and shaped by a number of ethical statements and guidance. More reflexively, however, what can be known about whom and how, the role of the researcher and the approach to generating data is, in essence, to determine the ethical stance itself. A stance of 'reflex reflexivity' (Bourdieu, 1999: 608) necessarily presumes that data is constructed and that research stems from a social relationship. This is a research directive which is, by implication, an ethical one. Matters of ethics underpin and were embedded within the research purpose, design, method, data handling, analysis, presentation of findings, and dissemination. What distinguishes research from other encounters and everyday interactions is its objective of generating data and creating knowledge. As such, I acknowledge my presence within the generation of the data, as well as in its analysis. It is an inescapable aspect for *all research*. It is in the consistency of the research design and the reflexivity of the researcher that the data and findings can reach transparency and rigour (Fine et al, 2000; Punch, 2005). Throughout, I conducted the research with an awareness of my position as a researcher and of my presuppositions in

5

a conscious way that directed me to be aware of 'those inevitable acts of construction and the equally inevitable effects those acts produce' (Bourdieu, 1999: 608).

I was motivated to conduct this research by an interest in the subject area, one which arose primarily from my previous employment in a children's voluntary organisation. I was also motivated by a desire to produce useful applied knowledge on an under-researched area, in a participative way. Recognition of the relational aspect of research necessarily also acknowledges the affect of conducting the research on the researcher (Coffey, 1999), and this has, at times, been a disconcerting subject to explore. I have also been conscious throughout all stages of this research of the significant personal and professional 'stake' in the findings from those who have invested in it. For various reasons, at times, I have wanted to shy away from my analysis. Contrary to the aim of some research, and researchers, I did not seek to immerse myself in the lives of others, or in the data. I did not desire to, or imagine I could enter the worlds of others in a way that would enable me to experience it or 'see' it as they do; neither have I considered that complete indifference or detachment is possible or desirable (see Coffey, 1999). I consider that the most productive analytical position, one which pays respect to the research participants and the data, is that which acknowledges the importance of distance and closeness. It is a position that recognises this tension within all aspects of the research process, but which also sees it as necessary if one is to conduct and produce 'good' research. It is this balance between distance and closeness that I have sought and attempted to negotiate throughout. In this way, it was the reasons that caused me difficulty which also motivated me to push for that rigour, outlined previously, to ensure that what I have produced pays respect to all those who were involved in the research.

Structure of the book

Chapter One sets out the historical and contemporary representations of CSE and the ways in which the terminology and definitions of the problem have changed within policy frameworks, and which have influenced and continued to influence how this issue is defined and responded to. This provides a context for the discussion that follows in later chapters by providing an analysis of the sets of ideas within which CSE has come to 'exist'; signalling toward problems arising from the current conceptualisation of CSE.

Chapters Two and Three explore the ways that young people and professionals made sense of why sexual exploitation happens. In Chapter Two attention is given over to the wider context surrounding young people's experiences, and why or how it is that some young people are vulnerable to being sexually exploited. The chapter considers that unmet needs are essential to a full understanding of CSE. Inadequate care (relationships, systems and acts), lack of opportunity for reciprocal relationships, unacknowledged agency and feelings of being object were considered to be at the root of the exploitative relationships and circumstances in which young people were involved. Chapter Three explores the different ways that the two groups of participants conceptualised young people's risky behaviours and risk to CSE. Drawing on the concepts of childhood and youth, the chapter considers the difficulties that the professionals displayed, and talked about themselves, in making sense of young people's agency and involvement in CSE, and considers how this was different from the ways in which young people made sense of (what is perceived by others as) risks and risky behaviours.

Chapter Four outlines the different ways in which 'CSE' was understood to occur. I consider how grooming may not always feature and, when used definitively as a model, is inadequate for understanding how sexual exploitation occurs. Building on previous discussion, this chapter considers how for some young people exchanging sex can be a coping response to other difficulties, and a way of feeling as subject. In considering these different models for understanding CSE, I argue that the element of *exchange* is fundamental to each, and suggest that exchange is what makes sexual exploitation particular and distinct from other forms of sexual abuse.

Chapter Five considers what the participants had to say about responding to CSE. This chapter considers the importance of recognition, reciprocity and interdependency – specifically in the context of care and care relationships – and also signals to the need to acknowledge the wider context surrounding sexual exploitation.

In the final chapter, I draw together the three key arguments made throughout the book. First, CSE is wider than the individual instances of sexual exploitation or sexually exploitative relationships, and 'care' (relationships, systems and acts) sits at the crux of the problem of CSE. Second, conceptions of CSE may be problematic for young people, particularly with regards to understanding and framing young people's agency, and I consider the implications that this has for responses to the problem. Third, intrinsic to CSE is the element of exchange, and underpinning this is the meeting (and exploitation) of unmet needs. I suggest how this approach provides a way of making sense of both young people's agency, *and* the abuse they experience, through exchanging sex. It concludes by arguing that the language and concept of 'CSE' is both narrow and narrowing, misdirecting the focus of the problem, serving to exclude some young people while also having serious implications for responses to and interventions for CSE and other forms of sexual abuse.

...and what is without

As with any study there are a number of decisions I could have taken and did not, and the focus and scope of this research are apparent in the discussion above. That said, before proceeding further, there are some notable absences from this book which deserve some mention here. The reader may note that gender and race do not feature significantly or much specifically in my discussion. The overarching aim of this research was to provide an in-depth understanding of child sexual exploitation and this has directed the research to a consideration of policy and practice frameworks, informed by theories around youth and childhood in particular. Accordingly, I did not make a feature of gender or race with regard to the subject matter. I am well aware that the de facto position within much of the rhetoric surrounding this issue is that it is a problem concerning girls. I am also aware that boys are represented disproportionately in much of the rhetoric and the literature on youth as 'trouble' (see Hebdige, 1988). In addition, I note that the prominent media reporting of the high profile cases mentioned in the opening lines to this introduction focused on the grooming of white girls by gangs of Asian men,[1] while matters relating to race and ethnicity are notable within the Jay report (see Jay, 2014). While it is important to acknowledge this, it is also for these very reasons that I have sought to avoid these 'givens' in the way the issue is typically constructed. This book is about hearing from and about young people with experiences of sexual exploitation. That said, issues of sexuality, femininity and masculinity, and race and ethnicity are key but it would not have been possible to do justice to these sizeable topics, and by that I also mean give full and proper analytical consideration to these areas, given the explorative design and inclusive focus of this study. Both are clearly areas that warrant much further research and commentary.

Note on the text

Finally, although this book considers data from young people *and* professionals, there is an important sense in which children and young people are central to the analysis provided here. Young people's visibility to others forms a part of the arguments threaded throughout this book: aspects of their being seen, people looking out for them, their recognition and acknowledgement are recurrent themes throughout. To 'see' is to look out for or look after, to understand, to recognise. *But how do we see young people? If we see them as children do we see them at all?* Consider the old and rarely heard saying 'children should be seen and not heard'. It is conventionally taken to mean that we should not hear from children; that what children have to say is not important. It has come to be understood as something we no longer agree with, yet it still has relevance, I think. We still want to know where our children are, we want to protect them, we are concerned to know they are safe; in this way, part of the saying is positively phrased – children *should* be *seen*, they should be visible to us. Yet how often do we really *'see'* children and young people? How often do we *really* want to hear from them, especially if what they have to say might not be pleasant, not something we consider as good for them – or not fit with our idea of what a child or young person should say? There are many ways in which some of the accounts considered here may sit uncomfortably with some readers, but there are many ways that children and young people experience CSE and, however uncomfortable, we should open up the space to hear and acknowledge this. For in order for a person to be 'seen' they must be heard; and to be heard properly there must be an acknowledgement that they are there in some authentic sense and that what they have to say is worth hearing, worth understanding.

It may be necessary before I continue to make it clear, as have others before me (see Montgomery, 1998; Piper, 2000; O'Connell Davidson, 2005), that while this book takes a critical perspective on child sexual exploitation, I do not in any way question the very real harms experienced by the individual young people whose lives are caught up in exchanging sex. I assume a position in which children and young people exchanging sex for something is a problem.[2] Given that starting point we must then ask what is the nature of the problem and for whom is it a problem. The reader may be relieved to know that while child sexual exploitation is the topic of discussion, they will find no specific details here about its occurrence. What follows is not some exposé of CSE. I have sought to provide a sober consideration of this issue; one which seeks to get behind the rhetoric about CSE, and open up its layered and contextual complexity. There is no search for simple answers, were these even possible. Neither is there any attribution of blame. Rather I have sought to provide a full and rounded understanding of this problem, in the hope that it assists in both an applied and conceptual sense, those seeking to do right by young people in such difficult circumstances, and those young people themselves.

Notes

[1] While I do not address race specifically, I do address throughout the book how the discourse of CSE is premised on and revolves around 'exclusionary conceptions' (see O'Connell Davidson, 2011: 454) of western childhood and adulthood (and citizenship). The depiction of the 'sexually exploitative Asian gang member' is arguably as mythical an image as the 'adult sexually exploitative predator' or the 'child seductress'; in that they each serve to reinforce and retain particular ideals and conceptions of the problem as belonging to some 'other' (see Chapter One for more on this).

[2] It is not within the remit of this work to consider whether the activity of exchanging sex per se for something is itself problematic, morally wrong or a concern – for literature that addresses this question one would look to the many sources that examine adult sex work and prostitution (see for example Spector, 2006; Doezema, 1998; Barry, 1979; Pateman, 2006). Notably, many of the authors who address the exchange of sex in relation to adults would typically argue that the issues for children and young people are fundamentally different (see for example Nussbaum, 1998).

ONE

From 'child prostitution' to 'child sexual exploitation': an overview

Children and young people abused through exchanging sex for something is not new. Neither is it new to societal, political or practice awareness. What is new is the current understanding and representation of the phenomena. While the introduction of 'child sexual exploitation' has been relatively recent,[1] it is important to note that the issue is directly rooted in 'child' or 'adolescent' 'prostitution', and has been the re-emerging subject of policy, practice and public concern throughout the late 19th and 20th centuries (see Brown, 2004; also Brown and Barrett, 2002). This reconceptualisation has formed a paradigm shift in how we understand the problem and those caught up in it – moving from an issue in which young people were positioned primarily as offenders of criminal or anti-social behaviour, to one where they are now looked on as victims of abuse. Yet this is not simple semantics. This change in terminology signifies a change in the meaning of the phenomena itself. Both terms – prostitution and sexual exploitation – are historically situated and conceptually loaded, creating theoretical boundaries to the ways the problem has been (and is) understood – and, as a consequence, defined in policy and practice directed responses (see Kelly et al, 1995). Children's agency, responsibility, blame, and conceptions of vulnerability are integral to the way this issue has evolved within policy and practice.

How has this change come about? Why was this even necessary – what is it about this issue that saw it excluded from definitions of child abuse, when these were first formed, and why so long for its inclusion? This chapter sets out the historical and contemporary representations of CSE, and the ways in which the terminology and definitions of the problem have changed within policy frameworks, and explores how each has influenced and continues to influence how this issue is defined and responded to. I aim to provide a context for the discussion that follows in later chapters by providing an analysis of the sets of ideas within which CSE has come to 'exist', signalling towards problems arising from the current conceptualisation of CSE. I have organised this chapter into four historical phases, providing an overview of relevant literatures relating to child prostitution and child sexual exploitation, situated within their associated policy and legislative contexts. It is not intended as an exhaustive historical account, but rather provides an overview of key perspectives, charting relevant key legislation and associated changes in practice responses as well as revealing shifts over time in the way the topic has been framed within selected literature.

'Child and adolescent prostitution': a problem for the bad, mad or sad

Prior to 2000, there was no clear separation between adults and children exchanging sex within legislation vis-à-vis the notion of prostitution. The legislation and responses in place for dealing with children and young people involved in prostitution were directed by the 1956 Sexual Offences Act and the 1959 Street Offences Act. While implemented in the 1950s, these were largely unchanged from those in place at the turn of the 20th century (see Brown and Barrett, 2002), and so the introduction to matters of legislation begins at this historical juncture (for a more developed overview of the legislative context at this time see Aitchison and O'Brien, 1997). These Acts set out how to deal with instances of soliciting and loitering for all those aged 10 and over (the age at which one can be held responsible for a crime). The Acts were gender specific. The 1959 Street Offences Act refers specifically to females and set out that any behaviours relating to 'soliciting' and 'loitering' for sexual purposes were deemed to be a criminal offence and punishable by law. This was dependent on proving 'persistence'. If it were proved that the activity had occurred more than once the female would be deemed by law as a 'common prostitute'. The 1956 Sexual Offences Act applied to males only, and set out that behaviours relating to soliciting in a public place were deemed to be a criminal offence. This Act did not define those behaviours as prostitution and there was no requirement of persistence to be proved. Responses to children and young people involved in exchanging sex or sexual activity for some form of payment were largely punitive, and a child or young person would be dealt with through cautions, fines, imprisonment or removal to 'safe houses' under the auspices of control and protection (Gillespie, 2005).

Although legislation prior to 2000 did not distinguish between adults and children, Gorham (1978) suggests that the *issue* of child prostitution became a social problem of some concern, if not panic, in the late 19th century when the journalist W.T. Stead in 1885 published his sensationalist accounts of children 'ensnared', 'kidnapped' and 'entrapped' into prostitution. Yet children and young people's involvement in prostitution was not some new revelation for society. Brown and Barrett (2002) provide a helpful analysis of the sexual standards of the time and the context for attitudes regarding prostitution. Women were to remain 'pure' until marriage, while the expectation for men was to be sexually knowledgeable. In this way, prostitution was tolerated and seen as a necessary evil to preserve the institution of marriage. This view was class based. Men's sexual knowledge could be safely garnered from the lower classes and not affect the expected sexual standards claimed by the middle classes, while also keeping marriages intact by the expedience of an alternative sexual outlet (see Jesson, 1993). At the same time the 'problem' of prostitution was related to morality and deviancy, and often cast as a feckless promiscuous girl being a threat to the innocent man, with the responsibility and blame falling on the (female) child, young person or adult (see Brown, 2004). So what was now different in 1885? Arguably, Stead's articles garnered sympathy among middle class reformers largely because of his emphasis on forced abduction – meaning that this was a potential problem for *all* children, and by definition those of the reformers too. Yet, as Gorham argues,

> had they allowed themselves to see that many young girls engaged in prostitution not as passive, sexually innocent victims but because their choices were so limited, the reformers would have been forced to recognise that the causes of prostitution were to be found in an exploitative economic structure. (1978: 355)

By focusing on a deviant adult 'other', the problem remained positioned outside the family and structural issues in society that cause difficulty for young people, so detracting from the fact that some children and young people were left with little choice or means to survive other than to exchange sex to meet their needs. In this way, the issue became located around mythical images of the child, as either a blameworthy seductress – an aberration of a child – or as an innocent, abducted and chained by an aberrant adult stranger (Ennew, 1986). Brown (2004) writes how the issue of child prostitution re-emerged in the interwar period as a result of reformist movements, such as the Association of Moral and Social Hygiene (AMSH) and the National Vigilance Association (NVA), which sought to push the attention and blame from children and young people to the adult male 'customer' – again drawing on the image of the abused, innocent, dependent young child as a way of garnering sympathy and support for the cause. However,

measures were as likely a response as protective ones was a very real issue: between 1989 and 1995 nearly 4,000 police cautions were given to young people aged between 10 and 18 – most of which were given to those aged between 14 and 18 years (see Ayre and Barrett, 2000). Brown and Barrett (2002) suggest that the response from statutory services was more likely to focus on controlling troublesome children, and there was a reluctance to initiate safeguarding responses, allowing criminal justice responses to proceed.

Prostitution as a survival strategy?

Research findings relating to child prostitution in the late 1980s did not come from a focus on child prostitution per se, but rather from research with other vulnerable groups of young people, such as 'young runaways', which revealed that prostitution was a survival strategy for a significant number of those involved in the research (see for example Newman, 1989). From this decade onwards there was a decisive shift away from a focus on deviancy and promiscuity, towards a consideration of the social and economic circumstances surrounding involvement in prostitution (see Cusick, 2002). Research findings began to show commonalities, such as the number of young people involved in prostitution who came from the care system (O'Neill et al, 1995; Shaw et al, 1996), were homeless or were in vulnerable housing situations (Kirby, 1995). O'Neill's (2001) three-year ethnographic study with young people 'on the street' was an attempt to move away from knowing *about* young people involved in prostitution through the sociology of deviance and criminology and to find out *from them* about their experiences. Findings from O'Neill's research are themes common to those indicated by other authors writing about the problem: young people involved in prostitution were found to have problematic relationships with adults such as carers, detached mothers and abusive male role models; were subject to negative stereotyping and labelling by caregivers and those working with them through criminal justice proceedings; were likely to have been subject to bullying and had experienced the care environment as something negative. Violence was a taken-for-granted aspect of their lives, and many had previous experiences of sexual abuse; many also had histories of offending.

Attention was also turned towards structural inequalities and poverty, and the few options for children and young people to survive outside of the home and care context (Shaw and Butler, 1998). As Green et al (1997) argued, the gradual withdrawal of young people's access to benefits and welfare meant that prostitution was often the only option available to some young people. Young people's lack of stake in society, the decline of provision and services for them, and the increase in punitive measures for young people who, for whatever reason, were out of the mainstream and refused to engage, meant that young people were left with no real choices (Pitts, 1997). In a first mention of 'sexual exploitation' as far back as 1986, Ennew (1986) argued that the sexual exploitation and abuse of children must be understood in the context of wider power relationships between children, young people and adults. Critical arguments challenging the framing of young people's agency and issues of choice and responsibility began to feature, with an emphasis placed on how prostitution is rarely devoid of complex circumstances and difficulties. As McMullen (1987: 39) outlined, for some young people, there are many reasons to exchange sex and no reasons not to – further arguing that 'socio-economic factors, unemployment experiences, educational experiences, attitude formations, confidence levels, family scapegoating' can all feature in the reasons behind young people's involvement. As Shaw et al (1996: 13) argued, in knowing that young people may not be forced, it does not then follow that they necessarily 'freely choose to enter prostitution'. Moreover, the concept of children and young people giving informed consent when they have no active citizenship is questionable (Kelly et al, 1995). In their comparative ethnographic study into the experiences of street-based young male sex workers in Cardiff and London, Davies and Feldman (1992) concluded that the young people involved in the research were not always pushed into sexual exploitation, but that 'sex work formed part of a street lifestyle in which the passing of time became an end in itself' (1992: 7). They further suggested that rather than understanding young prostitutes as necessarily damaged, uneducated and living in poverty, there was a need to acknowledge that some young people considered themselves to be exploiting economic opportunities they were presented with; opportunities which in their view were often better than the other means of employment available to them.

Another aspect of the problem brought to attention was the relationships young people had with 'pimps' and boyfriends, and the coercive element of involvement in prostitution (see McMullen, 1987; Kelly et al, 1995; O'Neill, 2001; Palmer, 2001). Within this body of literature came the concept of 'grooming' as a model for explaining the involvement of children in prostitution (van Meeuwen et al, 1998). 'Grooming' was the term used to describe the process whereby an abusing adult develops a relationship and builds trust with a young person through the provision of gifts and attention. Once that trust has been established, they exploit that trust and demand repayment or favours, in the form of sexual activity with themselves and/or others. With its language of 'ensnaring', 'total dominance' and 'perpetrators' (see van Meeuwen et al, 1998), the argument echoed back to W.T. Stead in 1885, and his emotive descriptions of 'entrapped' young people (Gorham, 1978), and attempts by reformers to locate the blame or responsibility away from children and onto some adult male 'other' by highlighting a young person's innocence and lack of agency (Brown, 2004). The model presented a compelling argument to challenge the punitive legislative direction by locating the child as a victim of an adult perpetrator, and it received attention from voluntary organisations campaigning to change policy and challenge societal negative stereotypes of children involved in prostitution.

Redefining prostitution and 'child prostitutes'

The increased knowledge regarding the reasons behind children and young people's involvement in prostitution informed understandings of child prostitution as something other than monetary exchange for sexual activity. One such definition often cited was that put forth by Green (1992: 5) who noted that children and young people can offer 'sexual services in exchange for some sort of payment, such as money, drink, drugs, other consumer goods, or even a bed and a roof over one's head for the night'. Others highlighted that some children exchanged sex for affection, friendship and trust (see Kelly et al, 1995). It was acknowledged that calling children 'prostitutes' could be stigmatising and was a form of negative labelling (see Melrose, 2004), and in the literature from this period there is a noticeable and often explicitly stated departure from references to 'child prostitutes', and the appearance of terms such as 'young people involved in prostitution' (Hayes and Trafford, 1997), 'children sexually abused through prostitution' (Barrett, 1997), or 'young sex workers' (Adams et al, 1997). Towards the end of the 1990s there was a significant campaign element to the literature that sought to redefine the issue itself to one of children *abused* through prostitution (see for example Barrett, 1997). As Shaw et al (1996) pointed out, the problem defined as child prostitution carries stigma and pushes blame onto the child, whereas understanding it as child abuse means that the focus and attention of punitive measures is redirected towards an abusing adult. This literature also began to question the legitimacy and effectiveness of the punitive measures brought against children and young people. The concern here was to position child prostitution away from its associations with promiscuity and criminal offending, and change the statutory response to from punitive measures to protective ones (see Brown and Barrett, 2002). However, such a discursive shift, as Adams et al (1997) showing a degree of foresight cautioned, the concerns for 'protection' that had come to dominate discussion detracted from the policies that created those conditions for prostitution. They warned that protective measures were likely to be perceived and received by young people in the same way as the current measures focused on control and crime prevention. They also disagreed with the campaign to re-frame the issue for children as one of abuse, seeing young people and children in the same way as adults, and different only in their marginalisation. They argued for the legalisation of prostitution, and that only a broader change in social policies centred on welfare for young people would bring about a real change. This view was also supported by Davies and Feldman (1992) who suggested that policy and legislation should be changed from a punitive approach to one that supports young people without 'exiting' being the end goal (1992: 2).

It was, however, the strength of argument and extensive campaigning from children's voluntary organisations that helped promote a change in legislation that heralded the beginning of the next phase in the issue's history.[4]

Children abused through prostitution: a new paradigm?

At the turn of the new century, as a direct result of some of the campaign literature described above, the UK government introduced *Safeguarding Children Involved in Prostitution* (SCIP) to re-frame policy and practice in England and Wales (see DoH, 2000). SCIP produced something of a paradigm shift by asserting that children – defined as all those under the age of 18 – involved in prostitution should be treated 'primarily as victim[s] of abuse' (DoH, 2000). Soon after, the 2003 Sexual Offences Act (DoH, 2003) introduced new measures relating to child prostitution aimed at targeting those who purchase sex from a young person and/or are responsible for enticing a young person to sell sex, by making these activities punishable by law (for a comprehensive overview of this legal context see Gillespie, 2005).

SCIP reconfigured child prostitution to a child protection and safeguarding concern rather than one of crime and offending. The document stated that child prostitution should be treated as distinct from adult prostitution on the basis of children's differences in capabilities. It also made explicit reference to changes in public awareness and to research indicating that children's involvement in prostitution was the likely result of coercion by an adult. This explanation was reinforced by the *Guidance Review to Safeguarding Children Involved in Prostitution* (see Swann and Balding, 2001) which aimed to review the practice progress that had been made since the introduction of the new legislation. This document is explicit in its mention of child victims, of adult perpetrators and of grooming as the explanation for sexual exploitation. The (re)positioning of child prostitution hinged entirely on agency and responsibility. Despite the new focus, SCIP stated that in cases when children *voluntarily choose*, or refuse help, punitive measures should still be enforced against them:

> The Government recognises that there may be occasions, after all attempts at diversion out of prostitution have failed, when it may be appropriate for those who voluntarily and persistently continue in prostitution to enter the criminal justice system in the way that other young offenders do ... Nothing in this guidance decriminalises soliciting, loitering and importuning by children on the street or in public places. The Government considers that the criminal law plays an important role in establishing society's view that "street prostitution" is not welcome nor is it acceptable for children to be involved in it. The law can act as a deterrent and a lever to use as part of a diversion strategy. (DoH, 2000: 10)

Children and young people involved in prostitution were defined as victims of abuse only if they were groomed or when they were unable to consent. As Phoenix (2002: 355) argued, SCIP served to 'merely redefine the problem while leaving intact the machinery of more traditional criminal justice responses'. Indeed, separating out a welfare response based on whether young people were persistent and voluntary, or coerced and abused, was, in the view of some commentators, likely to undermine the very purpose of the document (see Melrose, 2004). In this way, the document introduced something of a binary depiction of children involved in prostitution, simultaneously placing children both as victims of exploitation and offenders (Gillespie 2007; Moore, 2006), the difference being predicated on choice and persistence. Tellingly, the legislation did not seek to define what it meant by 'persistence' or 'voluntarily involvement' in order to allow professionals working with children to make their own decisions and interpretation of circumstances (DoH, 2000). Yet, as Lowe and Pearce (2006) argued, by continuing to polarise the issue, SCIP gave practitioners little encouragement to look beyond a young person's behaviour and explore the individual economic and social situations in which they may be. Concerns were also raised about the possible 'stereotyping of vulnerability' (Gillespie, 2007: 13). Indeed, a young person could be perceived as entirely capable and at odds with an expectation of what an abused child should 'look like', presenting a challenge to the victim concept (Brown, 2004) and their own status as victims. Rather unsurprisingly, the discourse within practice and campaign literature emphasised the victim status of children and young people, with a lack of agency, and of coercion and manipulation from adults in order to ensure that professionals dealing with the problem would initiate a care response rather than a punitive one (YWCA, 2002; Unicef, 2001; NSPCC, 2003; Taylor-Browne, 2002).[5] This shift occurred even as authors raised related concerns about how minimising and ignoring young people's agency may serve to undermine them further (see Lowe and Pearce, 2006; Moore, 2006; Pearce, 2007). Yet, as Melrose argued,

> this debate is extremely sensitive since if we are arguing that these young people are victims of abuse, there are certain vested interests in showing that they are involved in prostitution as a result of being coerced by an abusive adult rather than as a result of their own agency. (2004: 8)

It was in this time period that 'child prostitution' began to disappear within applied research, public campaigns and some practice circles. 'Child prostitution' was considered by some to be suffused in stigma and without explicit acknowledgement of the problem as a form of abuse (see Cusick, 2002),[6] and those changes in terminology discussed in the previous decade were superseded by a new discourse of 'child sexual exploitation' (see for example the 2006 issue of *Child Abuse Review*).

Understanding the problem

The research literature at this time tended to focus on the reasons behind young people's involvement in sexual exploitation in order to inform prevention and intervention practice. Taylor-Browne's (2002) interview-based study with 47 women who had engaged in prostitution when they were younger found that the reasons came primarily from an economic need arising from unstable housing situations. Once they had become involved in prostitution their involvement was maintained through incentives to stay, such as feeling there was no other option; low self-esteem; drug addiction; losing touch with people because of their life situations; and having no other support or help. Research also revealed insights into the prevalence of sexual abuse in childhood among sexually exploited young people, concluding that, for some, prostitution was a way of gaining control over their bodies (Pearce, 2006; Drinkwater et al, 2004). As Lillywhite and Skidmore (2006: 356) suggested, 'being paid or 'rewarded' for sex can feel like a big improvement on the sexual abuse they may have previously experienced'. Research also began to highlight the role of local authority care in the problem (see O'Neill, 2001; Pearce et al, 2002). Coy (2008), in her study exploring the life stories of young women selling sex, explored the links between local authority care and their experiences. Key findings suggest that the rules and arrangements of care, characterised by instability and disruption, combined with the additional experiences of abuse, family disruption, substance misuse and peer relationships were more likely to act as 'push factors' into selling sex. Coy (2008: 1411) concluded that the 'psycho-social experience of being in care affects young women's sense of identity and decision making processes', while responses such as placing young people in secure units were likely to increase their risk through an 'internalization of deviance and worthlessness' (2008: 1417).

Responses to the problem

Research findings were used to inform the development of 'risk indicators' or 'factors', to help identify children and young people who may be experiencing sexual exploitation. Pearce et al's (2002) study exploring the experiences of 55 young women experiencing sexual exploitation identified three categories of risk: those young people who are at risk of sexual exploitation because they face a number of challenges and are engaging in some risky behaviours; 'young people who are swapping sex for accommodation, money, drugs or other favours 'in kind'' (2002: 41); and young people 'selling sex' (2002: 55). Similarly, Coles' (2005) study in Wales outlined four categories of risk, on the basis that some young people's actual involvement might not be known: not at risk; at mild risk; at moderate risk; and at significant risk of sexual exploitation. These categories influenced practice by enabling professionals to assess a young person's risk level and areas in which they need support (see for example Clutton and Coles, 2007). Practice-informed research also highlighted that young people involved in prostitution may be chaotic, disruptive, challenging and hard to engage (Scott and Skidmore, 2006; also Melrose, 2004). The difficulties of working with young people who are sexually exploited, and young people's reluctance to engage with services were attributed to previous negative experiences with professionals, complex issues facing young people and the grooming process – which could mean that some young people either did not consider themselves as being exploited or were afraid to seek support (see Chase and Statham, 2005; Clutton and Coles, 2007; Pearce et al, 2002; Scott and Skidmore, 2006). Direct services and suggested forms of practice were developed on the basis that the causes behind sexual exploitation are multi-faceted and require a multi-faced, inter-agency response (see Kerrigan-Lebloch and King 2006). Research and service evaluations suggested that successful interventions should be based around outreach work. Barnardo's 'Four A's model' of access, attention, assertive outreach and advocacy (see Scott and Skidmore, 2006: 6) stressed the need for services to be available and accessible, to provide 'consistent and persistent' positive attention and to advocate with services to ensure young people get appropriate provision. Similarly, Pearce et al (2002: 71) suggested that therapeutic outreach and continually offered support, regardless of a young person's commitment to it, would demonstrate workers' commitment and avoid contributing to young people's experiences of rejection (see also Edinburgh and Saewyc, 2008).

'Child sexual exploitation'

The discussion now turns to the most recent history. In 2009, England and Wales launched separate guidance and child protection legislation, replacing SCIP.[7] Wales' guidance[8] was subsequently re-launched again in 2011 although much of the main content and the definition remains the same:

> Child sexual exploitation is the coercion or manipulation of children and young people into taking part in sexual activities. It is a form of sexual abuse involving an exchange of some form of payment which can include money, mobile phones and other items, drugs, alcohol, a place to stay, 'protection' or affection. *The vulnerability of the young person and grooming process employed by perpetrators renders them powerless to recognise the exploitative nature of relationships and unable to give informed consent.* (WAG, 2011: 9, my emphasis)

Under the new legislation frameworks 'children involved in prostitution' formally became 'child sexual exploitation', firmly establishing the problem as a child protection issue requiring only a safeguarding response. Recent research has been concerned with the lack of implementation of the guidance by Local Safeguarding Children Boards (LSCBs) and concerns over a lack of awareness of the problem among practitioners (see Clutton and Coles, 2007; 2008; Jago et al, 2011; Paskell, 2012). However, much of this research is based on data from LSCBs, and little is known about professionals' perspectives and understandings of child sexual exploitation (see Jago et al, 2011, for an example). Similarly, aside from two studies conducted in the 1990s (Davies and Feldman, 1992; Shaw et al, 1996), there had been no further research conducted in Wales on young people's experiences of sexual exploitation, or their perspectives about the problem itself. Research in Wales has been mainly quantitative, intended to understand the scale of the problem, evaluate the safeguarding protocol, and to summarise progress in awareness, practice and protocol implementation (see Coles, 2005; Clutton and Coles, 2007; 2008). However, this marked absence of the views of children and young people in research stood across the UK and remained for some time after the introduction of CSE policy and practice (see Warrington, 2010; also Pearce, 2009; Firmin, 2013, for examples of research involving young people). Concerns have also been raised that placing sexual exploitation as a concern of child protection may not be helpful for young people (see Pearce, 2009; 2010, Phoenix, 2010). Pearce (2010) argues that social work is geared towards protecting children from abuse within families, while concerns surrounding the lack of response to the needs of young people have also been connected to concerns about the framing of vulnerability among young people. As Jago et al (2011: 4) argue, a 'conceptual shift' is needed in social care to recognise older children/ young people as also at significant risk of harm. They go on to state that there is a need to challenge 'practitioners' acceptance of young people's apparent consent to abuse' (2011: 6). Yet, as Cusick observes, perceptions of young people's need and risk are inevitably related to people's understandings of the problem, stating that 'the legacy of traditional responses is likely to be with us' (2002: 241): a point which leads us to a consideration of that legacy and its implications for our understanding of the problem and how best to respond to it.

And so we have arrived at a problem now termed 'child sexual exploitation'. One which declares that no child can consent to their own abuse (see WAG, 2011: 11; DCSF 2009), which is explicit in its mention of grooming and which locates the problem not as the activity – the exchange of sexual activities for something – but as the (grooming) process of coercion and manipulation of children and young people. The increasing tendency within practice research and government reports to equate the problem to that of grooming is so much so that one could be forgiven for thinking that sexual exploitation *is* grooming (see Melrose, 2012).[9] The emphasis on the grooming process may be partly to blame for a confused use of the term CSE in public discourse. Child sexual exploitation is often used interchangeably with the term child sexual abuse, and has become the term used to describe any form of child sexual abuse occurring outside of the home and family. This is notably so in cases related to Operation Yewtree – with the focus on grooming in reporting of details surrounding investigations into those such as Jimmy Savile and Rolf Harris.

The grooming model was developed from practice experience gained over a number of years by children's charities working with children involved in prostitution/child sexual exploitation, and it is not the intention here to deny its relevance, however when presented as the sole explanation it homogenises the experiences of children and young people into a single story (Melrose, 2012). Just as the discourse in the late 19th century with its emphasis on passive innocent victims served to obscure the realities and circumstances for children and young people, so the current rhetoric around sexual exploitation is one that is in danger of continuing this (see Moore, 2006; Gillespie 2007; Melrose, 2012). As Phoenix (2002: 359) argues, 'grooming' arguably limits the 'theoretical space in which the full complexity of the lived realities experienced by some young prostitutes can be apprehended and explained'. Melrose (2010; 2012) further argues that the emphasis on grooming means we are in danger of continuing to distort the realities for children young people involved in exchanging sex by instead focusing the attention on abuser and abused. It arguably serves to detract from the economic and circumstantial reasons young people may be in, and the circumstances surrounding young people's involvement in exchanging sex, as well as allowing for only one 'route' into it (see Ayre and Barrett, 2000). Moreover, as Phoenix (2002: 365) argues, even when sexual exploitation occurs within coercive and exploitative relationships, 'grooming' de-contextualises these, reducing them to relationships in which young people will do anything 'for the sake of love'.

'Child sexual exploitation', defined in this way, locates the problem not as one where young people are 'involved in prostitution per se, or the social and material conditions that often drive young people – and then justify involvement in – prostitution'. The 'real problem' becomes the abusing men who entice or abuse young people (Phoenix, 2002: 355). As Day points out, the language surrounding sexual exploitation makes the complex entanglements of economics, gender and value appear unrealistically simple. There are abusers and abused: traffickers, pimps and victims. Such simplification discourages public debates on alternative action because it promises easy solutions as well as telling us what to think. (2009: 1)

Day's argument is one made with regard to discourses around trafficking among children and adults, but the point is very relevant. As Edwards (2004) observes, there is a need to understand the powerlessness young people experience in society and to consider the problem and how we respond not just in terms of sexual abuse, but in the wider social, economic and political context.[10] However, being now firmly established as a social care child protection concern, the problem is now framed within that particular field of policy and legislation. Boyden (2006: 197) argues that social work tends to look to the individual for the causes and the solutions, arguing that social work (with children) and child protection practice and legislation 'tends to play down the impact of wider social, economic, political and cultural conditions in the shaping of social phenomena'. Ideas of childhood and youth are central to this, which directs to a consideration of such conceptions in relation to the ways in which the problem of child sexual exploitation is understood.

The 'child' in 'child sexual exploitation'

Child sexual exploitation operates within a social policy field which posits children as being all those aged up to the age of 18 years. Moreover, 'child sexual exploitation' posits children and young people within a particular conception of childhood and draws on a particular construction of the child; in fact, its very existence (in its current conception) relies on this construction. There is no 'adult sexual exploitation' equivalent in UK policy, with the debate for adults framed in terms of sex work or prostitution (dependent on one's position on the issue). The new terminology of CSE may have evolved from abuse through 'prostitution' but its evolution has been such that its historical roots are almost unrecognisable. We have child *sexual exploitation*, because it is *child* sexual exploitation which relies upon a particular positioning and framing of childhood. In its current conception, 'child sexual exploitation' emphasises that children and young people who are sexually exploited cannot consent. They are sexually exploited because they are groomed, and it is *this* which places them as victims of abuse. In so doing this obscures young people's agency, defining them as helpless, but, as the history of this issue has shown, necessarily so because it is their agency which has been (and is) problematic. As Ayre and Barrett (2000) observe, child prostitution was the last form of sexual abuse where the victim was held as having some responsibility. In her study of 20th century constructions of child prostitution Brown considers how:

> over the twentieth century ... [t]he negative portrayal of child prostitutes as sexually knowledgeable and experienced, and the assumption of comprehension and choice on the part of the child have been instrumental in excluding child prostitution from being encompassed in definitions of child sexual abuse. (Brown, 2004: 345)

The problem of child prostitution has been focused around individuals and located within discourses of choice and responsibility, with conceptions of the problem revolving around binary, mythical images of the child as deviant and the child as innocent abused by an adult (Ennew, 1986). There has been little space for understanding the problem as being anything other than children being forced against their will, or voluntarily choosing to engage in prostitution. The former has been deserving of society's care as they cannot be deemed responsible, and the latter should be held responsible, are accountable, and so did not deserve support. In this way, consent and perceptions of children and young people's agency are fundamental to understandings of the problem and its current framing. Constructed as CSE is, there is now little space for understanding children's agency, while the grooming model leaves no room for any doubt about the young person's victim status because they are victims of predatory adults.

But this particular framing of the issue is problematic. There is a wealth of literature available that argues that 'childhood' and what is it to be a 'child' are constructed concepts (see Montgomery, 2009; Jenks, 2000; Lee, 2001). Where the biological differences between a five-year-old and a 15-year-old are fairly self-evident, the values ascribed to what it means to be a child, to childhood and to when that childhood ends are not (Prout and James, 2006). The binary conceptualisation of children involved in prostitution as dangerous and a potential menace, and as innocent in need of protection have their roots in Lockean and Rousseauian conceptions of childhood (see Valentine, 2004). The protestant Lockean conception is one of children as inherently sinful and in need of correction; whereas the romantic Rousseauian conception is of children as innocent beings who gradually become corrupted by society (see Kellett et al, 2004). Hendrick (2006) argues that policies around youth offending and those concerned with 'children as trouble' fused together these two opposing views by placing the construction of childhood within the family ideal. In this way, national interests were bound within conceptions of childhood through their related categories of parenting and family. Concerns for child protection and child welfare have their foundations in the Rousseauian view of childhood but with roots to the late 19th century and conceptions of universal childhood as a time for happiness and innocence (see Ennew, 1986). Brown and Barrett (2002: 37) argue that child protection is based on middle class values of early reformers and campaigners who sought to 'normalise the condition of childhood across all social spheres – characterised by removal from the economic sphere and from the sexual sphere. In this way, it is the 'demanding ideal' of innocent childhood, and the binary construction of children that has provided the 'rationale and purpose for both voluntary and state intervention' which focuses on care and control (Brown 2004: 346). As Shaw and Butler (1998: 180) argue, within the context of social care, 'powerful constructions of childhood and adolescence are predicated on the dependence and incapacities of children rather than their strengths and competencies'. Within social care structures and systems, children are seen as inherently vulnerable and there are a multitude of policies in place to safeguard and protect them and to minimise danger. There is limited attention given to promoting wellbeing and children's agency is primarily viewed as a threat or danger (Daniel, 2010).

Yet childhood is not 'naturally asexual' (Heinze 2000: 18, see also Edwards, 2004; Kehily and Montgomery, 2004; Renold, 2007). Neither are children passive non-agentic dependents (see for example Prout and James, 2006; Lee, 2001; James and James, 2004; James, 2009). The history of this problem has been characterised by a demonising of those who did not or could not conform to this ideal of what it is to be a child (Corteen and Scraton, 1997). This is something evident in the positioning of 'juvenile prostitutes' as offenders. And yet this framing of children is not confined to history. As Kitzinger (2006: 165, 1) has argued, there is a 'fetishistic glorification' of childhood, in which sexual abuse is constructed as a 'crime against childhood' as much as against an individual child. This can have the perverse effect of setting those who have experienced abuse or neglect as being outside childhood – and more so if the child or young person is perceived as being culpable in some way. Children and young people who deviate from those expected norms of childhood can become the deviant 'other', or 'non' child, perceived as somehow less vulnerable or more streetwise than other children (Kitzinger, 2006; Montgomery, 1998; Piper, 2000; Moore, 2006).

The problem of sexual exploitation, then, is one that has particular relevance for young people. In the UK certainly, it is young people mostly in their teenage years who feature most prominently in statistics and are understood to be more at risk of experiencing sexual exploitation than younger children (see for example Aitchison and O'Brien, 1997; Coles, 2005; Pearce et al, 2002; Pearce 2009); however, 'child sexual exploitation' may be problematic as applied to young people and youth as socially constructed categories. Youth is an ambiguous and interstitial status, distinct from childhood yet lodged somewhere between it and adulthood. As such, young people are not children any more than they are adults, or they are both; they are awkwardly placed, as Valentine has it:

> teenagers ... lie awkwardly placed between childhood and adulthood: sometimes constructed and represented as 'innocent' 'children' in need of protection from adult sexuality, violence and commercial exploitation; at other times represented as articulating adult vices of drink, drugs and violence. (2004: 6)

Policy and social problem concerns about youth and young people over the 19th, 20th and 21st centuries are in no way limited to those relating to child prostitution and matters of child protection. Young people are troubling and troubled in ways which link them to a wide range of all too familiar public anxieties – crime, poverty, violence, housing and homelessness, ill health, disorder – in which they not only figure as the empirical object of public concern, but also play a talismanic or symbolic role (see Hendrick, 2003). As well as being a problem *for* society, youth and young people stand as symbols of wider problems *in*, or *with*, society. Pearson (1983) provides a revealing history of the ways in which young people repeatedly feature in social anxieties about risk, unruliness and vulnerability, all the way back to the 16th century. Pearson's work stands alongside sociological studies on youth deviance and the problems of youth, the classic example of which would be Stanley Cohen's work on moral panics (see Cohen, 2002). Cohen's model has crossed over from its sociological home into wider social scientific and public discourse, and has been used to explain and contest the logic behind a number of sensationalist media and moral campaigns targeting identifiable groups and categories (folk devils) as scapegoats for wider, public anxieties. A relevant example here would be Jean La Fontaine's analysis of allegations of 'ritual' child abuse in the 1980s and early 1990s, which draws on both Cohen's moral panic model and anthropological theories of the social role of witchcraft accusations (see La Fontaine, 1998: 13). The reference to Cohen here, however, is more for his original study on mods and rockers and panics related to *young people* as scapegoats themselves, his argument being that youth and youth cultural forms provide an evergreen focus for moral panics in which teenagers come to stand for 'conflict, resistance and strife' (2002: xliv) thereby deflecting, and providing an outlet for, deeper uncertainties about social order.

As Hebdige (1988: 27) argues, 'the category "youth" emerges in its present form most clearly around the late 1920s' and its construction can be attributed to the tradition of ethnography within the Chicago School of social ecology.[11] Hebdige further argues that those classic works from within the Chicago School have left sociology with two particular enduring images of youth and young people: one of a social group in a period of vulnerable transition and the other of young people as delinquents who are a product of their (often degraded) urban environment. Images which can be easily discerned within the framing of young people involved in exchanging sex – in policy, public debate and representation, and the literature too. Hebdige belongs to the tradition of youth studies associated with the semiotic, political and ethnographic work which emerged from the Centre for Contemporary Cultural Studies (CCCS) in Birmingham in the 1970s. Notable works on youth cultures associated with the CCCS include Willis (1977), Hebdige (1979), Hall and Jefferson (1993); McRobbie (1991) (see Wulff and Amit, 1995, for a brief synopsis of this work). These sought to explore youth culture as something other than 'anti-social' but as necessary and sometimes oppositional attempts by young people to carve space for themselves within dominant social and ideological formations, to 'establish ... presence, identity and meaning' (Willis, 1990: 1).[12] Yet across all these studies and more, youth continues to figure as a relational concept, distinct from but existing only in relation to adulthood and childhood.

This understanding of youth as an interstitial phase is certainly an enduring feature of social policy literature on young people, where the term 'adolescence' can be found rather more than in the sociological literature, normatively understood as the time in which young people come to terms with their changing bodies, emerging sexuality, new forms of relationships, and new identities, as they leave childhood behind and enter adulthood (see for example Coles, 2000). '[T]he "discovery" of adolescence as a distinct transitional phase of life', as Montgomery indicates (2009: 202), can be traced as far back as 1904 and G. Stanley Hall's depiction of adolescence as a time of storm and stress. Wyn and White note the continuing influence of this way of seeing young people:

> 'youth' is associated with dependency, ignorance, risky behaviour, rebellion and a pre-social self that will emerge under the right conditions ... the concept of adolescence ... assumes the existence of essential characteristics in young people because of their age, focussing on the assumed link between physical growth and social identity. (1997: 12)

Sociologist Richard Sennett adopts something of the same position when he writes that 'adolescence is commonly thought to be a period of wandering and exploration' (1996: 14). It is this established and normative view that sees young people situated within social policy without the full protective rights afforded children (because no longer children), while not yet afforded the full rights of adults (because not quite yet adults either). They are both at risk and a risk; subject and object of the welfare state (see Smith et al, 2007). They have the responsibility of citizenship but are not given all the corresponding rights; while the problems that concern them can be largely ignored or subsumed into those of child policy (Dean, 1997; Daniel and Ivatts, 1998). Set within this wider context of welfare and social policy, and particularly so in a neoliberalist policy agenda with a focus on individual responsibility rather than collective social policies with a concern for welfare, making space for young people's agency is and has been problematic. As others have commented, it has been entirely possible to convict young people for offences in which they were not legally able to consent to taking part (see Pearce, 2009; Coy, 2016), while the current context for and understanding of CSE directs towards child protection responses that may not be appropriate for young people and at the same time detract from wider and more structural issues that contribute to the problem.

There is a long history to this problem, which is bound up in understandings about childhood and youth, and which has focused on individuals as both cause and solution. Young people's vulnerabilities, risk and risky behaviours, and their agency, are central to the framing and understanding of this problem; while what this problem is and how young people come to be caught up in it is also not perhaps as clear as first thought. It is within this context and background that the book now turns to consider such categories and concepts from the perspectives of young people with experiences of being sexually exploited, and professionals with experiences of supporting such young people.

Notes

1. As I will explore later in the chapter, 'child sexual exploitation' began to appear in social care related literatures in the earlier 2000s; however, it was only formally introduced to policy and practice guidance in 2009.
2. Maria Colwell's death brought about the first serious case review in social work. Neither Maria Colwell nor any part of the review are remotely related to concerns about child prostitution, but the review itself saw about what has been termed by Butler and Drakeford (2012) as the beginnings of a continuing 'crisis in social work', in which the values and purpose of social work, and individual social workers themselves, are continually subject to criticism and demands for justification.
3. This model could stand as an exemplar of the changes in understanding of this issue, especially when contrasted against the 'grooming' model (see later in this chapter).
4. Much of what I have considered as occurring throughout this era was also similarly taking place at a global level too, culminating in the Second World Congress Against Commercial Sexual Exploitation of Children (CSEC) in 2001 (see Saunders, 2005). Here too was a concern to action policy to support and help children and young people involved in prostitution and also pornography and trafficking. Although there are many parallels between the global changes in the depiction of children and young people involved in the exchange of sex, the development of UK policy relating to CSE has taken a distinct path from policies relating to CSEC internationally – which could in part be due to the latter's focus on movement and commercial trade, in the trafficking of persons and images across borders, by those crossing borders (tourists looking to exploit) and working across borders (criminal organised gangs): a difference that can be seen in the UK's policy and practice areas of trafficking and CSE, which remain distinct even though they are often positioned alongside each other and considered to overlap.
5. It is worth noting that, as an example, there were seven different protocols across the 22 local authorities in Wales, each with different definitions of child prostitution/sexual exploitation, and only one of these stated that punitive measures should be used as a last resort (see Clutton and Coles, 2008).
6. The importance of this point for some commentators can be seen in Goddard et al (2005: 278), who argued that to refer to 'child prostitution', or 'child prostitutes', was to commit 'textual abuse'.
7. There is no agreed UK definition of CSE, and each of the four nations currently have different definitions and associated guidance. I focus specifically on the Wales definition and guidance as a case in point, and because it provides the policy and practice framework surrounding the research findings and discussion presented in this book. Despite these differences in policy definitions, much of the language and directed practice in CSE related policy across the UK nations are similar.
8. *Safeguarding Children and Young People from Sexual Exploitation* (WAG, 2011) acts as supplementary guidance to *Safeguarding Children: Working Together under the Children Act 2004* (DCSF, 2004); and to the *All Wales Protocol: Safeguarding and Promoting*

the Welfare of Children who are at Risk of Abuse through Sexual Exploitation (which sits within part 5 of the All Wales Child Protection Procedures). Practice and guidance is directed by the Sexual Exploitation Risk Assessment Framework (SERAF), and operates on the basis of identifying established vulnerability and risk factors which correlate to a risk score. The score determines the risk category and its associated child protection action. Those scored at 'mild risk' require no formal procedures but work should focus on prevention, such as making the young person aware of risk and educating them about healthy relationships. Where the score is 'moderate risk' or 'significant risk' it should initiate a multi-agency strategy meeting where a formal protection plan should be arranged.

[9]   For example, the Child Exploitation and Online Protection Centre's (CEOP, 2011: 7) report into child sexual exploitation was based on findings from 'a thematic assessment of the phenomenon known as 'localised grooming' ... where children have been groomed and sexually exploited by an offender, having initially met in a location outside their home'. A report to the House of Commons Home Affairs Committee also explicitly equates child sexual exploitation to 'localised grooming' (see HCHAC, 2013).

[10] Here is another point at which the literature surrounding CSEC (or specifically trafficking) and CSE intersect. As Saunders (2005: 172) argues, the language of CSEC has developed out of a narrative of duped and trapped children who are at the mercy of western foreign tourists, corrupt business men or criminal gangs, in which the focus has centred on the 'corruption or loss of innocence' as the problem and concern.

[11] Cohen's is a landmark study but is hardly a point of origin. Sociological attention given to youth and young people can be traced all the way back to the beginnings of the 20th century at least.

[12] Moving into the 21st century, however, the sociology of youth shifted its focus away from studies of youth subcultural activity (which by the 1990s had become a rather more crowded and compromised field than in the late 1970s and 80s) and towards questions of the transition to adulthood and citizenship. Here the issues were less semiotic and spectacular but rather more ordinary – yet still troubling. Arguments begun in the mid-1980s in the context of high levels of youth unemployment developed into a wider questioning of the transition from youth to social majority which posited this as a more extended, complex and possibly fractured move than had been the case for much of the 20th century (see for example Morrow and Richards, 1996; Furlong and Cartmel, 1997; Dean, 1997; Fuller and Unwin, 2011). Young people figure here as immediate objects of concern but also, again, as talismanic of wider changes affecting society as a whole. Today, sociological studies of youth range across a vast array of topics. A glance through Coffey and Hall's (2011) three volume edited series on researching young people shows sociologists and others writing about young people and global and local mobilities, consumer identities, the negotiation of space and place, educational trajectories, substance use, sexualities, social exclusion, body politics and much more.

TWO

Vulnerabilities

Vulnerable (adjective): exposed to the possibility of being attacked or harmed, either physically or emotionally.
(Oxford English Dictionary)

This is the first of two chapters exploring the ways in which young people and professionals made sense of why sexual exploitation happens. In this chapter, attention is given to the wider context surrounding young people's experiences and why or how it is that some young people are vulnerable to being sexually exploited while others are not. 'Vulnerability', 'risk' and 'how young people experience sexual exploitation' are somewhat abstract and arbitrary as categories. Although analytically separable, and usefully so, they are interlinked and the boundaries between them are somewhat blurred. The distinction between these categories, however, reflects one made by both the young people and the professionals in the ways *they* made sense of child sexual exploitation; and it is a distinction made within policy and practice guidance too. As indicated in Chapter One, vulnerability and risk factors have been developed from research, and provide a way of enabling practitioners to 'see' sexual exploitation. They are the means by which professionals and practitioners working with children and young people can identify who may be at risk of CSE or experiencing it. Much of the attention within practice is on identifying and managing young people's 'risk' (primarily conceptualised as their risky behaviours) – something I turn to in Chapter Three. In so doing, these 'factors' also provide a narrative for explaining sexual exploitation, for they direct us towards an understanding of how and which young people come to be caught up in it.

The analysis here begins by exploring what the young people and professionals had to say about why they and others may be vulnerable to being sexually exploited. Many of the young people insisted that 'it' 'could happen to anyone'; however, it will become clear throughout that not just *anyone* could be sexually exploited. The young people referred to 'things going on', to borrow a phrase from Katie, standing to mean the difficulties, situations and circumstances they had coped with or were in, which meant they were vulnerable to being taken advantage of. As Nathan clearly tells us:

> **Nathan:** it doesn't just happen, it happens because either things just aren't addressed people are less able to fend for themselves and they don't get the help *they need,* for whatever reason, and are put into difficult positions and sometimes it *does* take them there and if, people were there to help them in the first place then they wouldn't, then this wouldn't happen

There are two aspects of the problem that can be glimpsed in what Nathan has to say: directly implicated in the problem are unmet needs, these 'things' that need to be addressed, and the lack or absence of help. Across all the professionals' accounts too was an assumption that there is some form of unmet need or circumstance which makes a young person vulnerable (and thus more at risk) to sexual exploitation.

Before I continue, as indicated in the introduction to this book, there is an important sense in which the young people's accounts are central to the analysis that features from hereon, and, that being so, it seems necessary to reintroduce them here. The details I give are sparse, in part because I do not wish to commit to them the same exposure through the revelation of intimate details that we hear them speak of in later chapters, but also because this book gives attention to *their* accounts in relation to events, time and place and are their ways of viewing the past and what for them made sense in terms of what happened. It does however seem necessary to give some context to those accounts. 'Young people' is a portmanteau category and I use the term with some care. They were aged 14 to 17 at the time of the research. Eight are female, and one male. While their histories and circumstances are varied they shared in the claim that they each had experience and some multiple experiences of the 'exchange of sex for some form of pecuniary reward or some form of material benefit' (Melrose, 2012: 159). While I acknowledge the diversity of their experiences – and we hear of those experiences in later chapters – it is this which brings a key commonality. In addition, they were all in receipt of support from a voluntary sector service for young people at risk of sexual exploitation; each had some past or present involvement with statutory social services; eight were or had been Looked After children (for two of them, this was as a result of their risk of sexual exploitation). As such, these eight had experienced periods of living in residential and foster care, or of living with different family members for periods of time.

The analytical focus is largely on participants' accounts, what they said, and less so on how they said it. Nevertheless, what they said cannot be completely divorced from the way in which they speak. Their narratives for the most part cannot be described as 'rehearsed'. The young people hedge, pause, are hesitant and appear to 'think out loud'. However, their phrasing, at times, appears to reflect the vocabulary of a social work discourse (see Jordan, 2004, for key features of this discourse) and may reflect the fragmented acquisition of a welfare argot from past encounters with various professionals. All the young people were at different stages of 'distance' from the situations they talked about and some were not distant at all. They were all in various stages of receiving statutory and/or voluntary support and the care experiences they described were either ongoing or recent. Some had been removed from risk situations (such as being placed in 'out of county' foster or residential care, or they were in secure accommodation). Some were being supported to remove themselves and to 'stay safe' living independently. Accordingly, none could be considered – or considered themselves – to have fully 'moved on'. In short, these were young people making sense of exploitative relationships or circumstances in which to varying degrees they were still involved. It is to that sense making, and to theirs and the professionals' accounts about 'things going on' that may be why young people become caught up in exchanging sex, that the analysis now turns explore.[1]

Instability: 'home'

All the young people spoke of their lives in terms of instability and insecurity. Many talked about the importance of home as a physical space, and most talked explicitly of having nowhere to call 'home', and in so speaking, they invoked an idea of home and an absent sense of safety, security, stability and belonging. Several talked of unsettled home lives and of experiencing frequent care placement moves and of an uncertainty about when or why they were moved:

> **Sarah:** this isn't *my* home, it's their home, I don't even know how long I'll be here. You just want to get out, get away you know.

> **Katie:** I was in care and I was moved around here and there and anywhere. So I was always doing runners, and then

> when I met [name of person deemed to be exploitative]
> it was having someone who was there for me you know.

Implicit within both these statements and a sentiment echoed across all the young people's accounts is an uncertainty about their 'place' and where they belong. For the young people, of importance is the *idea* of home rather than the accommodation itself. Their talk of "going missing" was related to this absence of home as a place of safety and belonging. As we can see in the views of Katie and Sarah above, "getting out" and "doing runners" were linked to the instability and insecurity of their care placements. They were not at 'home' and did not want to be where they were so they ran away. These feelings of insecurity and instability were related in the views of some young people to a lack of control or ownership over decisions about their care. As can be noted in Sarah and Katie's accounts above, it is not necessarily just the changes in care placements which can result in feelings of insecurity but rather, also, the sense that, like other young people 'looked after', they were not consulted about how and when changes to their care would be made. These experiences of constant change informed an expectation of it, and that they would not be in control of it. As Katie explains (above), she was moved to different residential units, "here there and anywhere", but this was not what *she* wanted. This point is also evidenced in Claire's observations below:

> **Claire:** then I had a male um social worker, and he told me I had to do, the video conference with the police, and I haven't heard anything about that ever since, so I've still got that going around in my mind, and I've asked um oh I've got a new social worker in but the third social worker, told me that she's coming down to visit but now it's been 5 to 6 weeks that I haven't heard from her. Now I've got a new social worker coming in that I haven't seen yet. I'm hoping she'll be an improvement.

We can see in Claire's account that she has little control or ownership over when she will see her "social worker" – a role performed by seemingly serial practitioners about whom Claire has no knowledge (or recollection) of when they will appear next. 'Home life' and aspects associated with it was described by the young people as characterised by instability and uncertainty and an aspect of their lives over which they had and felt themselves to have little control. The professionals' narratives bear many similarities to those held by the young people in this study. Family and the home were routinely implicated by many participants as having an important role in understanding young people's vulnerability to sexual exploitation. An aspect of common sense reasoning by professionals was that young people who have an unsettled or unstable upbringing were likely to have a sense of insecurity that could leave them exposed to exploitation:

> **Cathy (fostering):** Just insecurity, um um just not having a good, structural home base behind them, I think *home* is a massive thing and families are *huge* for security if the young people don't have family security at home then, you're just then like wallowing in not knowing where you belong, trying to find someone who could accept you so you do things to be accepted [pause] whereas when you're secure and accepted within your home base then there's less need to do that

Cathy's reflections are typical of many adult participants. Young people missing a sense of 'place' or 'home' were understood to have an absent or inadequate grasp of safety, security, stability and belonging – the emotional necessity of which they were considered to try to (re)create in negative ways (see also Pitts, 1997). Young people in care were spoken of as being particularly vulnerable for these reasons, because statutory provision of care was understood to be intrinsically unstable. Many professionals spoke of care as "unsettled", involving "frequent placement moves", in which young people may experience a number of "placement breakdowns".

Family and relationships

The young people also talked about instability and insecurity in reference to their relationships with their families and carers and those tasked to help and care for them. Across all interviews were frequent and repeated references to a lack of people to trust and an absence of people to care for or help them. As Danny and Sarah explain, they did not have anyone to help them when they needed help:

> **Danny:** like I wanted to get out of there [pause] no one would take me you know

> **Sarah:** I didn't have no one to trust really. There's no one there. No one is going to come and help, you know

The young people spoke about how they felt vulnerable because people would not listen, were not to be trusted or were not interested in them. They described feeling ignored and overlooked, invoking a sense of an absence of 'real' relationships with significant figures. This is similar to findings from Coy's (2008: 1415) study involving young women selling sex. Coy explains that the young women's lack of trusting relationships gave rise to a sense of uncertainty about themselves and an ontological insecurity. Without a web of relationships, they felt invisible. This sense of 'invisibility' is one that characterises these young people's narratives about the absence or inadequacy of relationships with people who care for and care about them. They were invisible because they were of note to no one. We see this expressed rather forcefully by Claire:

> **Claire:** my mum actually walked in and she didn't notice it [Claire communicating with an exploitative adult on the internet]
>
> *Sophie:* and she could have but wasn't looking for it or didn't notice it?
>
> **Claire:** yeh, basically, no one would acknowledge *me,* because as the term says with adults, children are like basically don't speak uh what is it?
>
> *Sophie:* um, do you mean children are seen and not heard?
>
> **Claire:** *yeh,* that's it basically, but it's like the other way round, which is, *don't be seen, don't be heard*

As Claire explains, she was not acknowledged by anyone – she was not visible and indeed she was *not* to be seen or heard – she should not *be* visible. Similarly, across all the interviews, references to not feeling wanted, feeling isolated, feeling unloved and having no one to talk to or with were prominent, and made manifest the importance of positive relationships that is echoed so clearly within policy and practice discourse. Here, "family relationships", "neglect" and "lack of positive relationship with a protective, nurturing adult" are likewise prominent in official accounts about the nature of vulnerability (see WAG, 2011: 15–16). Indeed, the young people were arguably 'vulnerable' in two ways in that they had not just practical unmet needs but unmet emotional needs – needs that we all have – the need to feel visible, acknowledged and to connect to people (Sennett, 2003;

Jordan, 2004). This was echoed within the professionals' sense making – albeit theirs was a reasoning that this is a vulnerability particular to children and young people (and not necessarily a universal one). All the professionals spoke of young people's emotional neglect and lack of positive attention from key people in their lives. A sense of ontological instability was talked of as arising from young people's relationships in which those without a sense of 'family', of interdependencies and relational place and belonging were vulnerable. They spoke of concerns about young people who have low self-esteem, who are isolated, and who lack confidence – feelings that were understood to stem from being unwanted, rejected or neglected by their families. Many spoke of concerns about young people without a trusted adult. While there was a reticence within many of the accounts to talk of family, they spoke of problems in families in which there was a breakdown in communication, for reasons such as substance or alcohol addiction, or physical and mental ill health. These were families in which parents may be *present* but *absent,* in that they may be incapable of meeting young people's emotional needs. In this way the professionals' talk is arguably influenced by attachment theory – and the need for young children to have a strong relationship with a parent or 'significant other' in order to have a 'healthy' emotional and social development (see Bowlby, 1977). However, their concerns did not centre just on families. Again, young people in the care system were understood to be particularly vulnerable:

> **Cara (children's residential care):** I think it's because they feel rejected, from their families and that's why they're in care anyway, and, so they're looking for someone who'll love them [pause] I think that that's the main thing ... in Germany their care home system is *much better* and more effective like theirs is based on a more like *loving* approach, where they're very warm you know *cuddles* and stuff like that is *normal* it's like a *normal* family, and it works well over there and I think, like I don't see why we can't do that, because the main problems the main cause of all their problems, whether it's bad behaviour or just *aggressiveness* it's I think it's just down to that really, so if they were having just care and love from us, um, they wouldn't, they wouldn't really *need* to go out and find, criminals and paedophiles to give them that, that's what I think

Many professionals referred to problems within statutory care in which young people may have multiple and frequent changes in social workers and foster carers, or not have the opportunity to develop established secure relationships with those operating in loco parentis. They spoke of young people having a number of different social workers or people in their lives with whom they had little interdependent or reciprocal connection. Young people's vulnerability to sexual exploitation was understood to be linked to their unmet emotional needs to feel cared for and loved. Cara's perspective was fairly typical. Young people who have an "emotional void", "unmet emotional needs", and "emotional vulnerabilities" were understood to be vulnerable either because they will look to fill this void elsewhere, or they will be vulnerable to abuse from people who can provide some sort of attention, for good or bad. The implicit or explicit point is that this 'void' cannot be filled by those working in professional caring capacities with young people. Overall, relationships with professionals were considered to be unlikely to provide the time, continuity and commitment needed to be a 'significant other' in respect of a young person's emotional needs. So while these may be young people who have a number of different professionals in their lives, they are understood to receive little attention and to be isolated.

Sex and relationships

Many of the young people talked about negative sexual experiences and confused sexual boundaries as "important reasons" for why sexual exploitation might happen. We can see in the following passage that Katie was unsure about what was 'normal' sexual activity:

> **Katie:** Family is important you know, like my mum worked in a massage parlour and when I was living with my mum my dad used to shout at me 'your mum's a fucking prostitute, that's what you're going to end up as'. Like I thought it was ok I didn't know any different. That was normal to me you know.

Selling sex was perceived as a possibility by Katie, as something 'normal', because of her home experiences of living with her mother. Katie goes on to say:

> **Katie:** Sex definitely. That's definitely a reason. Like from a young age I was dabbling in sex from when I was quite

young and you think oh well this isn't such a big deal it
cheapens it a bit like it isn't so bad.

Katie's perception is that sex is, or can be, 'cheap' and meaningless, so it
cannot be somehow intrinsically 'bad' to experience sex in the way that
she does now. To Katie, sex is now of little consequence because it is
no longer of much value or worth. Yet Katie rather emphatically states
that this kind of sex is "definitely a reason" for her later experiences
of exchanging sex. If sex were still "a big deal" *to her* then it would
matter how she would want to experience it. Other young people also
talked about having confused or diminished sexual boundaries because
of previous abusive experiences of sex:

> **Hannah:** because of what happened with my dad, uh, you
> don't really uh you think it's just all normal...

Hannah was unsure about what was "normal" to expect or to feel.
She later went on to explain that she did not feel in control of her
body and talked about feeling "uncomfortable" with some kinds of
sexual activity but of not feeling "able to say no". She thought 'things
weren't right' but did not trust her own feelings about it. Similarly,
other participants spoke about how they had felt "used", and that sex
was something they did not have control over or always associate with
pleasure. As James (2000) argues, the body is the medium through
which people encounter social relations and, as such, it is intimately
connected with subjectivity and an authentic self. The young people's
confusion over sexual boundaries and practices was inevitably bound
up in their sense of self and their ability to control events, to even
control their corporeal selves.

Experiences of sexual abuse is recognised in the practice literature
which notes that 'Children who have experienced sexual abuse have
already been through a grooming process which establishes as 'normal'
a breaching of appropriate sexual boundaries' (Clutton and Coles,
2007: 20). Yet, notably, reference to previous experiences of sexual
abuse and to negative experiences of sex does not appear to feature
as a vulnerability indicator within extant policy guidance. Instead it
is couched within 'family history of abuse or neglect' or 'disclosure
of sexual or physical assault followed by withdrawal of allegation' (see
WAG, 2011: 15–16).[2] There may be good reasons for this. As discussed
in Chapter One, early research into 'adolescent prostitution' focused on
the links between childhood experiences of sexual abuse or promiscuity
and prostitution (see for example Davis, 1978). These studies tended

to pathologise young people – in which early 'sexual knowing' was understood to corrupt children and young people, turning them into 'abnormal deviants' (see Cusick, 2002: 234; Brown, 2004; Brown and Barrett, 2002). Such a view was not what the participants shared or intended. Rather, they considered that their experiences of sex had contributed to an uncertainty about their bodies and about sexual boundaries and this was understood to be an important reason for their later experiences of exchanging sex.

Again, this was a point that aligned with much of what the professionals had to say. Many spoke of concerns about young people having "distorted" ideas about relationships and sex from having experienced emotional and sexual abuse themselves, and/or having observed domestic abuse in the family home. They spoke of concerns about young people's limited worlds and realities, in that these negative relationships which young people see and experience will be understood by them as being 'the way things are' (Jenkins, 2004):

> **Martin (education):** I think that how people grow up has a huge impact on how they, well, view the world, the options that they see that are possible, and, they would see that as one of the options that is viable, that's how people are, they repeat the pattern, and then it becomes harder to break it. I would assume, that for girls growing up, with a mother who is a prostitute, that, if it seems to be working, and that's the model that they see, then, why would they *not* assume that that's a viable route for them to go down

As with Martin, many professionals talked specifically of their concerns about young people's understandings of the place of sex within relationships. Many related this to the inappropriate expectations and "unhealthy boundaries" held by young people about physical touch and affection. This was mentioned particularly in regard to young people in care who may also have previously experienced sexual abuse, in part because of the boundaries of touch and physical affection that exist in care relationships which can also be understood to be 'inappropriate' because of their restrictive highly bounded nature. In care, all displays of physical affection can be seen as 'inappropriate'. As Cara and Jack explain:

> **Cara (children's residential care):** because *we* as like workers can't touch the children *really* in any kind of caring way like if I see a child crying which I have I'm quite happy

to put my arm round them and comfort him but you can't really just generally just hug kids as you would your own

Jack (youth justice): Care homes are not establishing ways of dealing with young people that exist in normal loving homes

Jack, like many other participants, spoke of how professionals, particularly those working in statutory care, can find it difficult – impossible even – to display physical affection (see also Rees and Pithouse, 2008). As such, 'care' was understood to reinforce those confused boundaries of touch but also of relationships, as discussed above, which are unlikely to be open-ended and unconditional as in many families.

Exclusion

The young people also spoke of experiencing a lack of stability because they had been excluded from what they considered to be the 'normal' experiences of peers. They spoke of not having been in school like 'normal people', and how they did not have 'normal homes' or live like 'normal families'. Below, Leah expands upon this point:

Leah: if you go to school that's really important. You know it just keeps you around normal people do you know what I mean [pause] it's like rules and people telling you what to do. At the time I didn't think that was a good thing but it is, believe me.

Like Leah, all the young people talked about the importance of staying in school, and the reasons given were not linked to the need for scholastic achievement. School was considered to be a place that provides "rules"; that is, it provides boundaries and structure. As Leah explains, school is a place where "normal people" go. The young people talked about how they had been excluded (or had excluded themselves) or disengaged from school and stated that had they stayed in school their lives would have been better because they too would have been 'normal'. As can be seen below, this narrative thread of 'being like a normal person' was linked to other areas of their lives as well. Danny explains there are age appropriate experiences that you have "to get through" before you should "start living" and if a young person engages in "living" before they are old enough then they are not "living life how it's supposed to be":

> **Danny:** yeh go to school do it all, get through it and then afterwards you can start living do you know what I mean, you know be clean. Like I've done it all when I was younger, which I shouldn't have done. Like on my 18th I went to a pub and I was like oh I've done all this before, you know [pause] just live life how it's supposed to be, at *your age*, don't try and be older or younger than you are, just live it like you are supposed to live it…

Living life like a 'normal child' is to draw on a powerful normative sentiment about childhood (see Lee, 2001; Montgomery, 2009). The power of this sentiment is clear here. A sense of some regret about not having age appropriate childhoods was notable in several accounts, as was a consequent sense that they considered themselves to be 'outsiders' excluded from a 'normal childhood' and from the things that normal people do. This can be seen in Danny's talk where she refers to being "clean". To live like a 'normal child' is to *be* a 'normal child'. We also see this more emphatically stated by Katie:

> **Katie:** If I had gone into foster care I would have had structure. I think it would have been better, I would have been better, it would have been like a more normal child. You're thrown in the deep end with residential and you've no chance.

Katie considered that being in foster care would have given her the structure of an ordinary family life. As Katie states, she would have been like a "more normal child". 'Normal people' were considered by the young people to have structure and predictability. Normal people have 'rules', 'times' and 'boundaries' as a guide to help them, whereas the accounts of the young people suggested they were 'left' to work things out for themselves. There was no one there to help them. It is this which as Katie explains, means that young people with similar backgrounds to her 'have no chance'. This sense of exclusion and of being *something other than normal* is not captured within policy and practice guidance. 'Exclusion from school and unexplained absences from school' features as a risk indicator within Welsh Government policy guidance (WAG, 2011: 16), and CSE practice guidance also states that:

> Children and young people who are not engaged in school, who are isolated from positive social networks and who stay out late spend a large proportion of their time away from appropriate adults and protective networks. They are exposed to situations in which they are accessible to those who wish to harm or exploit them. (Clutton and Coles, 2007: 23)

So while there are some evident similarities regarding school as a protective setting, and policy and practice guidance of course uses different language to the young people, policy emphasises the 'risk' of young people outside of everyday structured settings, such as school, because it leaves young people less visible to the gaze and protection of 'positive nurturing adults' (WAG, 2011: 16). The risk or concern here is of the external other. Yet the young people spoke differently about this, talking of their feelings of being 'outside' of the mainstream where they were without reference to the social conventions that shape practices and subjectivities of what they deemed to be 'normal' lives. They were of course not wholly outside these structures of normalcy but by their sense of exclusion from key primary socialising institutions of family, school and positive peer networks, they perceived themselves to be 'outsiders' of a kind: somehow different, without protection or help. This difference in the framing of exclusion by the young people and policy discourse is one evident in the professionals' accounts too.

'There was no one looking out for them'

The professionals too considered young people to be vulnerable when they are out of the protective gaze of adults. Many professionals talked about young people who are "in the system" but who are not especially visible to social services, in that they had few if any positive relationships with professionals who might be expected to be looking out for them. They had no one in their lives who would question the suitability of a young person's friends, where they went, what they were doing. That said, participants considered how some parents may be ill-informed about risks and not able to see grooming that may be occurring. Others described how parents may be "stretched" by many responsibilities and lack support themselves, and as such unable to monitor their children effectively. They also spoke of how there may be 'poor or a lack of parenting within difficult families', in which young people are unseen and unobserved:

> **Louisa (social work):** I think the issue was maybe more their vulnerability, and the *lack* of um, kind of parenting, and the support they *or* the lack of any kind of support or family network, and I think, that they were probably taken advantage of, because there was no one out there looking out for them and so no one would know if they went missing.

Yet from what or whom would some young person be missing? The young people talked of by professionals were thought to be unobserved or overlooked by significant adults in their lives. Likewise, as noted earlier, the young people too felt themselves to be unheard and unseen. 'Young people going missing' is established within policy and practice guidance as a risk factor (see WAG, 2011: 16), and is one that is well noted within the literature (see Melrose et al, 1999; Pearce et al, 2002; O'Neill, 2001; Sturrock and Holmes, 2015). Yet, arguably, the problem is not just that young people 'go missing', because, as both the professionals and the young people explain, there was no one from whom they could *go* missing: the *problem* is that no one would miss them. As Annette explains:

> **Annette (third sector):** I *felt* quite strongly that *the circles* that they moved in it was those young people that they sort *of latched on* to the sort of party people, who had *no one else* that there was no one, *no one* who would *know* that they had been up all night, smoking cannabis, there was no one who would be going to miss them when they didn't turn up, for whatever, school, college, or for work, that there was no one that would ever *know* and it was *those* I think that were latched on to, I think that the kids that were living at home and having difficulties were not as vulnerable, the kids that were *still going to school* were not as vulnerable. These were the kids you know again the sort of kids that no one would *really care*, and I think from the start they can *see* the culture then of what their lifestyle *was* and those were the ones, who were ripe for the picking then because, *no one cared*

As discussed throughout, the young people considered to be vulnerable arguably have many people in their lives. Indeed, there may be too many people engaged with them: young people can be vulnerable because they are notionally of concern to a number of professionals but are of not much notice to any one worker in particular.

Andrea (healthcare): they're on their umpteenth social worker who say they can't care for them, but their actual behaviour isn't being addressed, and their needs aren't being addressed, and [pause] they are so desperate for uh for normality really but they end up putting themselves in very vulnerable situations 'cos nobody can protect them from them [those who exploit] and neither can they themselves

Implied within Andrea's account and noted across the data from other adult participants was that they, and other professionals like them, struggle to meet the needs of the children and young people they are working with. They acknowledged that this can leave young people looking for the sorts of care, relationships and attention that any person needs, and thereby become vulnerable to people who might exploit them for sex. The importance of this difficulty becomes evident when considering what the young people had to say about the people who took advantage of them, as is apparent within Katie's recollections:

Katie: I was in care and I was moved around here and there and anywhere. So I was always doing runners, and then when I met [name of person deemed to be exploitative] it was having someone who was there for me you know ... He looked after me. He gave me everything. Everything I didn't have you know. I was safe there

Katie was with her boyfriend because he was someone who was there for her – he *looked after her* – and gave her a form of care, stability and safety that she did not feel when she was in residential care. A revealing synopsis of the problem is given by Chris, who, perhaps unintentionally, reveals the crux of the problem (my emphasis in bold):

Chris (police officer): You know we, we have seen *fairly* early on, that yes we've got a fairly hard core group of looked after children, and **these LAC kids, are vulnerable because they are looked after children,** and they try *hard* to engage with the children to set boundaries, to to make them aware, of risks, but um, in every case you will find, there is some vulnerability, whether it be, they feel unloved, they feel ignored, or they have needs that are unmet.[3]

The redundancy of this phrasing signals an essential truth – 'these LAC kids are vulnerable because they are looked after children' belies an irony that to be a looked after child can sometimes mean being anything but. Paradoxically, to be a looked after child, as understood by both sets of participants in this study, is to experience a *lack* of care, attention and acknowledgement – a lack of that which is needed for anyone to feel perceived as an authentic and integral other.

These words offer a sharp contradiction in which to make sense of both participants' understandings of the problem. 'Care' – acts, systems and relationships – sits at the crux of why it is that some young people may come to be sexually exploited, while other will not. Such young people (without and within formal 'care' settings) can be overseen in many ways by different carers and professionals involved in their lives. Yet while they are visibly placed in care settings and encoded in official records, many remain outside the informal structures of care and attachment deemed protective of most children, and essential for them too. To be overseen in this way is to be looked upon but also to be looked over, with a surface attention that can feel superficial, leaving a child or young person feeling unacknowledged as an individual; missed, while not being missed at all. The notice they receive from the many different professionals in their lives can be experienced by young people as their being *objects* of concern, subject to surveillance – yet *beneath notice* in terms of a recognition of their subjective selves and inner world.

In its legal formulation, care relates to 'a dangerously circumstanced child ... judged fit for official guardianship', hence 'local authority care'. Since the Children Act 1989 the term 'looked after children' has typically been used to make reference to children whose care arrangements have them living away from home and under the supervision of a social worker. Both sets of participants aligned experiences of official care and being looked after with the problem of child sexual exploitation when talking about where the problem starts. This can be applied to both sets of participants' understandings of a young person's vulnerability regardless of whether they may have the legal status of being a looked after child. It is worth reiterating here that all the young people who took part in this study had experience of local authority care and several of them were 'looked after' young people. Every professional spoke of 'young people in care' as those who were most at risk, vulnerable and likely to experience sexual exploitation. This is also consistent with the literature, in which young people in care are noted as an 'at risk' group (see O'Neill, 2001; Pearce et al, 2002; Scott and Skidmore, 2006), and young people in or who have been in care feature highly in statistics related to adult sex workers (see Coy 2008). As O'Neill (2001) has argued, 'care' can be a vulnerability factor in itself (see also Shaw et al, 1996; Melrose et al, 1999; Pearce et al, 2002; Coy, 2008; Shuker, 2013; Hallett, 2015), and yet this is unlikely to feature in occupational statements about the management and reduction of risk, nor in public discourses around the problem.

The role of 'care'

It would be wholly remiss to suggest that only those in care or with involvement from local authority care can be sexually exploited; just as it would be to infer from this that all children in care are likely to be sexually exploited. Indeed, family, school and other key institutions featured within both sets of participants' accounts in terms of understanding how young people can become vulnerable to being sexually exploited. Experiences of being 'in care' can be understood as being at the sharp end of this understanding, but care and vulnerability should be understood more broadly.

As both the professionals and young people explained, a young person's vulnerability stems from complex causes and can be compounded through a number of factors that can (if unintentionally) render young people feeling as object. The young people spoke of themselves as being vulnerable, stemming from complex causes and compounded through their lack of stability and security – their feelings of not 'belonging' and a lack of 'home' gave rise to a sense of uncertainty about *themselves*, not least through their exclusion from what they viewed as 'normal', particularly their lack of trusting relationships and negative/abusive experiences of sex. They talked of uncertainty and a lack of consultation with themselves about the decisions being made about their care or reference to them and their ability to set the terms of their care and support, leaving them feeling insecure and powerless, uncertain of their ability to exert choices. Without a sense of 'place' and meaningful and positive reciprocal attachments they were unseen, blotted out, because they were without interdependent relationships (Jordan, 2004). Indeed, there were, paradoxically, *too many* people involved with some participants. These were professionals and carers whose relationships were unlikely to be open-ended or unconditional, but driven more by the canons of child protection and surveillance. In this sense the young people were watched by many but noticed by no one. Thus their sense of social and emotional exclusion impacted on them subjectively. Repeatedly, throughout their accounts, are references to 'normal people' and 'normal children', 'normal ways of doing life', a normal childhood that they had not or did not have access to and were excluded from. They *felt* themselves to be excluded, to be different, vulnerable, unnoticed. This was reinforced by their perceived lack of people to trust and help them. They were outsiders to 'normal life' and they felt of little notice to people who might care, and to the affect and relationships that 'normal' people take for granted (Coy, 2008). Their powerlessness, of not being seen to have an integrity of self that could assert choices or rights, also stemmed from feeling a lack of 'ownership' over their own bodies. As such, these vulnerabilities were compounded in that they were not recognised. Similarly, there were a number of factors related to young people's emotional wellbeing which were understood by the professionals to render them particularly vulnerable to being sexually exploited. They observed that it was those young people who were not paid sufficient attention, who lacked interdependent relationships, and were without key adults to notice them and acknowledge them both physically and relationally who are especially vulnerable.

This raises a further issue, just as troubling yet just as necessary to consider. As O'Neill (2001) argues, power and authority in the relationships between adults and children/young people needs to be examined when looking at why the latter might become caught up in or turn to exchanging or 'selling' sex. This is to acknowledge a wider societal frame not much recognised within policy (see Day, 2009). While the policy discourse surrounding child sexual exploitation does recognise the role of power and control, it does so only in relation to a grooming process between individuals (see Chapter One). Yet 'grooming' can, and needs to, be understood as taking place within, and as shaped by, a much wider context of established relations of power and control, command and subordination between adults and children and young people; relationships within which children and young people can sometimes (and also expect to) feel unheard, unnoticed, as object.

In this way, while it may at one level be controversial to state that social care and child protection can be harmful to young people, the provision and practice of care and protection devolve from a cultural framework of understanding and relations of power between adults and children and young people that can also compound the problem when care is experienced as something in which young people can feel unheard, unnoticed and unacknowledged. Care and protection (as something administered *to* those who are vulnerable, on *their behalf*, without *reference* to them), can unintentionally render young people as objects, contributing to their vulnerability, exposing young people to risk even as it seeks to shield them. As Ennew (1986: 140–1) has argued, 'the sexual exploitation of children is less a set of abnormal practices than an extreme manifestation of prevailing social and sexual values'. If we are to fully understand sexual exploitation, it must be understood in the context of power relations between adults and children/young people, and our *gaze* should turn towards the key institutions within which these relations operate.

Vulnerabilities

To return to Nathan's assessment of the problem, heard in the opening to this chapter, sexual exploitation does not just happen. For the young people, the reasons why they and other young people may exchange sex are bound up in a broad conceptualisation of vulnerability. They spoke of universals, in which any *person* – young or old – could be vulnerable. To return to my opening point, their insistence is that any (young) person can become caught up in sexually exploitive relationships and encounters if they too are facing and dealing with the sorts of difficulties, circumstances and complex issues relayed by the young people and outlined in this chapter, and are without means of help, support, care. The professionals' every day and circuitous constructions of vulnerability were different to those of the young people and similar to the ways that concepts of vulnerability and risk are applied within social policy relating to children and young people, whereby 'vulnerability appears simultaneously to be conceptualised broadly and narrowly with a view that all *children* are vulnerable, but some are more vulnerable than others' (Daniel, 2010: 235; my emphasis). There are, however, striking similarities in the ways that both sets of participants made sense of how young people come to be sexually exploited, why some young people are more vulnerable and thus at risk to those who would sexually exploit them. Underlying the many reasons why young people may become involved and remain in sexually exploitative relationships and encounters are unmet needs and a subjective self which can, at times, be denied. This is essential to any full understanding of sexual exploitation.

Emphasising the importance of unmet needs, the 'things going on' as the young people phrased it widens the lens on our understanding of the problem and directly connects it to those difficulties and the lack of support to address them. Yet as Pearce (2009) argues, there is little other way to understand sexual exploitation other than as individual problems and events. While 'vulnerability indicators' are present within policy, they are there as a way of enabling professionals to assess young people's risk to sexual exploitation (see WAG, 2011). They do not feature as a discourse to help explain the problem itself because the theoretical space in which to understand young people's involvement in the exchange of sex is limited to that of the coercion and manipulation of children and young people by (primarily) adult men (Phoenix, 2002). As we have heard, sexual exploitation is bound up in the complex 'messiness' of the everyday lives of those who experience it. 'Vulnerabilities' can be understood as extrinsic factors that can impact on a person subjectively – rather than intrinsic factors hinging on a (normative) understanding of the inherent vulnerability of children or young people, and one which is dependent on the very sorts of sentiments that the young people directed us to earlier in the chapter. This conception of vulnerability to sexual exploitation rests on an image of childhood as characterised by (sexual) innocence and dependency; a conception of vulnerability that by implication can exclude the very young people, such as those in this study, who are involved in exchanging sex (a point that I specifically return to in Chapter Five).

Alongside a recognition that children and young people lack the social, economic and relational power that adults have (see Ennew, 1986), conceptualising vulnerability in the way that these participants did positions unmet emotional, social, economic and/or practical needs at the centre of why it is that sexual exploitation becomes possible and where the problem starts. Understanding vulnerabilities as unmet needs also turns our attention to considering how young people may be attempting to meet those needs or deal with those sorts of vulnerabilities, how others might exploit these needs for sexual activity, and what consequences all this may have for how we might respond. Which is where the discussion now moves.

Notes

[1]   All participants names used are pseudonyms.

[2]   This raises the curious inference that those young people who have made a disclosure but have not later withdrawn it are somehow not at risk.

[3]   LAC stands for Looked After Children.

THREE

Risk

Risk (noun): a situation involving exposure to danger; the possibility that something unpleasant or unwelcome will happen.

Risky (adjective): full of the possibility of danger, failure, or loss.

(Oxford English Dictionary)

In this second of two chapters exploring the ways that young people and professionals made sense of how and why sexual exploitation happens, the discussion moves to a consideration of 'risk' and 'risky behaviours' in the context of those vulnerabilities previously discussed. Young people's risk to sexual exploitation is central to a contemporary framing of CSE. Alongside vulnerabilities, risk indicators are used in practice as a way of assessing a young person's likelihood of being or becoming sexually exploited; in this way they stand as a framework of sorts for understanding how it is that young people come to be sexually exploited. While theories of risk would seem to be central to a chapter made up in this way, they are not. Risk in this particular context stands to mean young people's actions and behaviours. For example, in UK government policy, 'risk' purports to mean 'the things that young people do' which indicate their likelihood of being sexual exploited, and risk indicators are defined, in essence, as young people's behaviours which can result in them being 'exposed to situations in which they are accessible to those who wish to harm or exploit them' (Clutton and Coles, 2007: 23). Furthermore, explanations for young people's engagement in 'risky' behaviours are often underpinned by attachment theory or conceptions of youth as a distinct transition phase from dependent childhood to independent adulthood; one embedded within normative western ideas of youth that carries associations of risk taking and rebellion as an expected and natural part of teenage years (see for example Foley et al, 2004). Directly implicated in this conceptualisation of risk is an understanding of young people's agency. Drawing on the concepts of childhood and youth, I consider the difficulties that the professionals displayed – and talked about themselves

– in making sense of young people's agency and their risky behaviours in respect of involvement in CSE, and how this was different from the ways in which the young people made sense of (what are perceived by others as) risks and risky behaviours. I begin by considering what the young people had to say about the things they did that they reflected on as making them more directly vulnerable to sexual exploitation.

Risk or resilience?

When the young people spoke about how they came to be sexually exploited, they did not typically talk about taking risks, or of the sorts of actions and activities that feature within CSE risk frameworks. While they talked about 'hiding away', 'hanging out', alcohol and drugs, and sex – behaviours that align with other research and with the risks outlined within policy and practitioner guidance – these were talked about as ways of coping with those 'things going on', how they felt and the situations in which they found themselves, outlined in the previous chapter, albeit sometimes made relatively unthinkingly. As I also considered there, these coping behaviours – or 'risks' – have been separated out from 'vulnerabilities' and 'sexual exploitation' as categories, but it is important to re-emphasise that they are intimately connected. Life is 'messy' and to understand events and actions as linearly presented is to misunderstand its complexity. As I consider later, young people's risky behaviours can be understood as resulting from a blend of self-assertion and inadequate support and care in their lives. These ways of coping were described by the young people as important and essential to any full understanding of sexual exploitation, not least because they direct to a particular understanding about where the greatest risks for them lie.

'Hiding away and hanging out'

The young people all talked about hiding themselves away, in both physical and metaphorical ways, as a means of dealing with the emotional turmoil in their lives. In relation to the former, some participants talked about 'locking themselves in their room', 'staying in' and 'keeping themselves to themselves':

> **Danny:** I was quiet a lot, I stayed in and wouldn't go out, you know the only time I would go out was in the night, and that was stupid because that's where I got into the mess,

> I don't know, I wouldn't go out in the day, I was only out
> in the night, going on my own for walks

Danny's account reveals something of the contradictions that appeared in several interviews with the young people. Danny tells us she was isolated, lonely and needed people to talk to, yet she hid herself away from people. Feeling isolated, she isolated herself further by hiding away or going out alone for walks. More generally, the young people spoke about how people cannot be trusted and in consequence they hid the 'inside person', the 'real' person from others. Hiding them*selves* and their feelings from others was a way of protecting themselves from further upset:

> **Claire:** If the family is ignoring the child, they need someone to talk to and they'll just go online and talk to people they don't know really, just for someone to talk to um … if your parents acknowledge that you're locking yourself in your bedroom and not coming out unless you're coming out for food or meeting up with your group, that's the other sort of suspicious way of realising that there is a family problem

Claire hid herself away from her family by staying in her bedroom. But while she was hidden at home she was 'out' via the internet – a source of people, often strangers, to talk to and be acknowledged by. As Claire explains, talking to strangers 'online' was a way of protecting herself in that she was hidden, she *could be anyone* and the people to whom she talked did not know who *she* was. Similarly, Nathan talked about how he had not 'come out' about his sexuality because he had no one he trusted to talk to. He explained that it was because of this that he went online to talk to people. The internet provided a way of protecting himself because he could selectively disclose aspects of his self without revealing his identity.

For many of the young people, hiding away to cope with feelings of isolation and insecurity also involved strategies for being acknowledged, seen and heard. Some participants spoke about 'hanging out' with peers yet hiding their subjective self by being relatively hidden within a crowd. They also talked about the importance of 'the group' because they gained a sense of membership and belonging, even if this were conditional and a surface form of belonging (see Wyn and White, 1997). For example, Leah talked about hiding her more vulnerable 'inside' self by aggressive acts to get respect from people:

> **Leah:** it's like there's this inside person and the outside person. And um, how you feel on the inside, you do things, and people might not know. 'Cos you look all hard and that. Like I had a reputation for fighting, so I get respect but then people don't know what you're really like, on the inside.

Leah explains that there is the person she is 'inside' that people *don't* see, and the person she is on the 'outside' that she invites people to acknowledge. Other participants explained that being with a group means not having to be or show your 'real' self. Young people who appear to have a 'network' of friends and peers (positive influence or not) can enjoy the bonding capital of social relations (Wyn and White, 1997) yet also retain a sense of isolation. The price of membership of the group is often to endorse values and demonstrate loyalty while sometimes hiding a sense of distance or disdain for group activities. The emphasis on overt displays of support for group norms (Willis, 1990) allows space to hide an inner self (McMullen, 1987). Yet, their sense of belonging in the group was always conditional:

> **Sarah:** you're out with your group, because there's safety in the group. I'd be hanging out with them 'cos it's a place to be. But then you've got to do things to keep up with everyone, otherwise they might think you're not bothering with them no more. You can't always trust people in your group.

Thus when Sarah describes how 'there is safety in a group' but also says that 'you can't trust people in your group' these are not contradictory claims but part of the nature of group life and how we accommodate to the collective and how we accomplish a careful and sometimes watchful membership (see also Jenkins, 2004: 70). In this way, the young people considered themselves (and sought) to be invisible in various senses and they nonetheless wanted to belong, and to feel part of something in some way.

Alcohol and drugs

The young people's accounts also revealed a widely shared invocation of the utility of alcohol and drugs as a means of coping. They spoke of how 'being drunk' or being 'on drugs' gave them confidence to do things they wouldn't normally feel able to do:

Sophie: Do you mean drinking can mean you don't have control?

Danny: Yeh well I don't anyway [laughs] you know, you wake up in someone's house and think oh my god where am I how the heck did I get here you know [pause] I think it's um, you can feel confident when you're drunk and think oh *whatever*, nothing is going to happen to me you know [pause] like I'd never walk down a back alley when I'm not drunk but when I'm drunk it's just, you know, just you do. Cause you can.

As Danny explains, she can *feel confident* when she is drunk, and she *can* walk down a back alley when she is drunk. When she is drunk she can feel like nothing bad is going to happen. McMullen (1987) suggests that 'streetwise' young people may have a warped perspective of the control they have over situations, which can lead them to take risks and place themselves in more harmful situations than they otherwise would. Yet the young people did not talk about getting drunk or taking drugs as a way of 'taking risks' and they did not speak of believing themselves to *be* in control by 'getting high' and getting 'drunk'. Drinking alcohol and taking drugs provided a way of *feeling* in control. As Willis (1990) argues, it is necessary to move away from received and truncated views of so called 'anti-social' behaviours to consider the alternative meanings these have for those involved. Young people's lives are 'full of expressions, signs and symbols through which individuals and groups seek creatively to establish their presence, identity and meaning' (Willis, 1990: 1). As Sarah explains below, alcohol and drugs provide a way of asserting one's presence:

Sarah: Alcohol influences you, you know, so you don't know what you're doing, same with drugs, it means you don't care anymore, you don't know what you're doing and you don't have to think about anything. You think you can do anything.

Drugs and alcohol can be a 'good thing' because they help Sarah to not know what she is doing while providing a way for her to think and feel that she can do anything. As such, they provide a way to *not* have to *think* or *care*. In brief, drugs and alcohol were talked about as providing a way for the young people to escape or forget their feelings and emotions and hide these from themselves and others. Getting high and getting drunk was a way to distance themselves from feelings, situations and relationships, thus providing 'an existential freeing of the self' (Willis, 1990: 102).

> **Kerry:** I think that everyone can be hurt and everyone can feel. It's like it doesn't matter what age you are. Yeh like alcohol if you're feeling bad then you drink too much alcohol and then you don't know what you're doing and you feel like you can do anything. Do you know what I mean? But then you get yourself into, trouble [pause] so I think choices and that, they are always connected to how you feel inside in some way

As Kerry explains, drinking alcohol is a way of coping with how she feels. It might get her into trouble, but it is *a* way of coping. In this sense, the accounts of these young people reinforces the relevance of guidance which states '[t]he relationship between sexual exploitation and substance misuse is a complex one which may include the use of substances as a coping mechanism' (Clutton and Coles, 2007: 23). The young people's use of substances was a way of coping with their feelings. It provided both the opportunity to feel in control of their lives – albeit for a short period – while also enabling them to forget about their feelings of loneliness, isolation and need to feel in control, or powerful in some way.

Sex and 'promiscuity'

Another way in which the young people sought to 'establish their presence' (Willis, 1990: 1) was through sexual encounters. To follow on from observations made in the previous chapter, while sex was experienced by some young people as a 'blotting out' of themselves as subjects, it was also a way of reasserting the self. Danny, below, talks about having sex as a way of coping with her experiences of being afraid to say no to sex:

> **Danny:** that's the important one, how you feel about yourself, that's where I go wrong you know I go around sleeping with everyone just to you know because I just didn't feel, good about myself, after it all happened, I just didn't feel good about myself, it's quite important you know [long pause] I dealt with it by sleeping with people, a lot of people, and I think it was because sometimes I was afraid

to say no, and then that's how I ended up dealing with it all like, it's about coping you know, like, you're just prepared to with anyone for anything like.

While seemingly paradoxical, negative experiences of sex and of 'sleeping with everyone', was a way for Danny to assert herself as subject. As expressed by other participants, it was a way of feeling in (some) control, of dealing with negative feelings and coping with the way they felt inside (see also Lillywhite and Skidmore, 2006; Clutton and Coles, 2007). 'Sleeping around' is a way of being in command of their bodies and them*selves*. Katie provided a similar view:

> **Katie:** you think oh well this isn't such a big deal it cheapens it a bit, like it isn't so bad. I may as well get paid for doing it.

Katie considered that sex had become something that had little intrinsic value. To get 'paid for doing it' was to (re)gain authority or ownership over her experiences of sex by reasserting her own (commercial) value to it. Sex can provide both a way of dealing with negative feelings and of asserting themselves as individuals. As Hebdige (1988:31) argues, 'if teenagers possess little else, they can at least own their own bodies. If power can be exercised nowhere else, it can at least be exercised here'. This is intimated in Hannah's reflections below:

> **Hannah:** I was *so* lonely at the time, nobody was listening to me or anything like that and I think part of me was like sod it, and that's why, stuff started and I ended up in trouble.

Hannah's sense of social isolation, of having no one who would listen to her, was in her view the spur to asserting her external self – to use her body as a way of being, as a way to become heard and seen.

Risk, resilience and resistance

It is important to note that the behaviours and attitudes discussed above were not claimed by young people as them somehow making 'rational' choices. Rather, they shared insights into how they were dealing with their lives without necessarily thinking about particular consequences. As Hannah explains, when she does these things, she isn't invoking some set of formal rationalities in which to weigh up life decisions:

> **Hannah:** how you feel about yourself because I, I've, you don't actually really feel, how you feel about yourself, until it's all, it's all over and done with, and you're why did I get myself into all this mess why did I do this why did I do that, so I think that's more or less after, it all happens [pause] you're not really thinking

Hannah, in common with all the young people, did not think about the more immediate or long-term consequences of her actions. Hannah did not think about 'the mess' that she might make. In part, because the purpose of doing the things they did was to *not* think (see Willis, 1990). Nonetheless, their existential horizons were not somehow of the moment only and several participants recognised a problem deferred, as Leanne suggests:

> **Leanne:** you end up digging a bigger hole for yourself

In ways that resonate with Pearce's (2009) research findings, Nathan spoke of a lack of support and feelings of social isolation as undermining resilience and as likely to precipitate the sorts of problems at the heart of this book:

> **Nathan:** It all depends on, the type of like support of the individual. Like I mean [long pause] the more supported they are even though they have issues it can [pause] they have something else, someone else to turn to, you know. Whereas I think the more isolated you are the more you do what uh can be taken advantage of. Like the more issues you have the more vulnerable you can be and that's that. I mean, if someone has just one thing then they should be more likely to be able to cope it's like [pause] I don't know it's like [pause] if you imagine each issue is like a little like, taking a brick out of a WALL, and you have to have something to try and support it support that wall. Um, the more issues you have the more gaps you have and the wall will crumble, um and that's when you fall into it [pause] and I think that's, that's the way you could see it

The tendency to drift into difficulties because of the absence of some significant positive figure(s) is explained by Nathan as a gradual almost inevitable spiral into difficulties and danger:

Nathan: No one addresses the diff like I said the difficulties that they *face*. Um, and, sometimes given that they *know* something bad is going to happen, their emotions just kind of go, I *need* this, um, because no one's been there to help *them*. They [pause] then they just turn to what's available

The young people acknowledged that this drifting into difficulties may be self-destructive but it is still a way of coping, and perhaps the only way. With a lack of acknowledgement, recognition and *care*, the young people found ways to feel present, and to help themselves in ways and means available to them. As such, Pitts (1997) theory of drift provides a useful way of conceptualising their accounts. Pitts emphasises the significance of young people's social isolation and their lack of a social network to provide 'support and solace' and 'which might ordinarily serve to prevent their drift into self-defeating or self-destructing behaviour' (Pitts, 1997: 149). It is this isolation set alongside socioeconomic disadvantages experienced by many vulnerable young people which can lead them, subjectively, to find ways to 'experience themselves as active agents' within behaviours which might otherwise appear as their actually lacking control or informed choice (see Pitts, 1997: 151; Melrose et al, 1999; O'Neill, 2001). Another way of understanding this is to consider that, within the context of the vulnerabilities and difficulties described in Chapter Two, for many young people, the only control they may have is to control how *out of control* they can get. Thus while practice literature makes clear the dangers of risky behaviours, it does not quite grasp the ontological insecurities and common sense rationalities that push young people to seek and assert agency. To cope by not coping at all. It is these understandings of risk that are not quite grasped by the professionals either. There are distinct differences in the ways in which the professionals made sense of why young people come to be sexually exploited, and to foreshadow later discussion, a difference which is perhaps bound to their understandings about what sexual exploitation *is*. The discussion now turns to a consideration of the professionals' reflections about what they considered to make a young person 'at risk' of being sexually exploited, and the ways they made sense of young people's risky behaviours.

Predatory adults and those who exploit

All the professionals talked about how young people are at risk from males who are looking to exploit. They did not speak of women in this way. Some spoke of clever, manipulative, predatory adult 'paedophiles' and 'sex offenders' – those who would be able to successfully target and single out vulnerable young people:

> **Trevor (policing):** their [young people's] vulnerabilities are *immediately* evident to the adult paedophiles

Other participants spoke more of 'sad pathetic older men hanging round' and 'silly young boys'. These were considered to target young people not because they are young, as a paedophile might, but because they are more easily manipulated. This was particularly so among those who spoke of sexual exploitation as occurring among young people. As Matthew explains:

> **Matthew (youth work):** it is, 'if you want to sleep with a girl then get em, get em, out of it', it's that age old thing isn't it, um, so these girls hang round with these older boys and I think most of them, you know they're 17, 18, but when you're talking about 12-, 13-year-old girls, the concerns sort of come in really [pause] *there are*, within this area you've got the [road name] crew, you've got some of the boys that, now they are sort of 23, 24, and you can't help sort of thinking oh come on now, you know, with 13-, 14-year-olds, why don't you just go to the pub like the rest of us, you know, stop hanging around on the streets, you're a bit old for doing this, can't you get anyone else

All the professionals talked of concerns about the places young people 'hang out', and their subsequent visibility to, and/or association with people who could exploit them. Young people are visible targets by nature of their appearance and likewise the spaces in which they congregate. Participants spoke of concerns about internet chat rooms, young people out on the street, or hanging around outside pubs or fast food outlets, young people in local authority residential care, and those living on their own in vulnerable housing:

> **Andrea (healthcare):** It was to do with places that she, would *hang out*, and she was associating with people who, were probably, just weren't holding things together but there was that veneer, in uh people have uh older people when they have problems they are able to have that veneer of respectability to give to a younger child who thinks, oh

they're alright they can look after themselves, she he then becomes associated with drug use and sex workers and, um, somebody who had been looking after her, worked in a massage parlour, so, if she's in that milieu she's not going to escape it

This is also a similar conception of risk to that within CSE policy frameworks, which emphasises concerns about young people who are outside of structured settings such as school, living independently and failing to keep in touch with workers, and young people going missing, are all established as risk indicators. The professionals' accounts echoed these sorts of areas. It is young people who are less visible to the gaze and guidance of protective adults, and their subsequent exposure to those who wish to exploit them, who are most at risk.

'Sexual experimenting' and promiscuity

All the professionals expressed concerns about young people who, in their view, were inappropriately sexually active. Many shared their anxieties about the sexual values and practices among young people, speaking of 'concerning sexual behaviour', uncertain sexual boundaries and 'blasé attitudes' towards sex. Linked to this they spoke of their concerns about young people's understanding of relationships and young people's understanding about the role of sex within these. The views expressed by Dave, Sandra and Marie are typical of those held by most participants:

> **Dave (fostering):** she'd had so much experience of going out and getting drunk and being used that it doesn't mean that much to her anymore

> **Sandra (education):** the ones that we see that say I've been sleeping with this person that person this person that person and that person I'm worried about in terms of their future, of the choices they're going to make, in life

> **Marie (third sector):** they could say no but they can't. Because they think that to get people to like them is not to say no to them

Their anxieties about young people's risky sexual activity were related to the age young people were having sex and the possible physical and emotional health consequences of this. Underpinning their concerns were normative understandings of sexual knowledge related to age, against which young people were understood to be going through a period of sexual experimenting, when their 'hormones' combined with exposure to the (previously hidden) sexual 'world' creates potential risk:

> **Carla (children's residential care):** I could see she was like getting into boys and all that now trying to, 'cos she's been exposed now to this world she wants all of it

> **Polly (youth work):** you know it's that sexual high tension time of experimenting and stuff, you know they have all these hormones flying around

In this way, many of their accounts could be considered to be loosely informed by child development theory, in which sexuality is considered as something emergent that happens during a period of growth rather than something which is somehow learnt and culturally mediated (see also Edwards, 2004). Many concerns spoken of by participants were related to how a young person's emerging sexuality is managed:

> **Andrea (healthcare):** young people have this *view* of paedophiles as being dirty old men in macs who go after very young children and they don't see themselves, as they're emerging into their own sexual selves, they see themselves as quite adult and so you have this sort of middling population who are, um [pause] emerging um and discovering their own sexual identity and yet that can be preyed upon and exploited, and they don't see themselves as potential victims because 'they are so grown up' and *then they are*, and so you get that um, they have physical maturity before they have psychological maturity and they are therefore quite vulnerable, and not able to defend themselves sometimes I see that, and I don't know whether that's to do with children being sexualised or pressure from their *peers*, and all the rest of it but there's something that um there are children that um who's *boundaries are just not there*, and for lots of girls it's very exciting to get lots of attention from older men, and it's a bit of a joke sometimes, and you can see how it's a bit of a joke a bit of flattery and then it all gets very serious, and it's very difficult to step out of

As with Andrea, other professionals spoke of concerns about young people's physical and sexual development which may not be on a par with their (assumed) emotional development. It is this that was understood to be the reason why young people can be at risk – and put themselves at risk – from those who may exploit them. They may be experimenting before they are ready to cope with sexual experiences, they may not have learnt appropriate sexual boundaries, they may be pressured by peers who may also be sexualised too early. Without the mature ability of foresight, young people cannot see that what may seem to be fun can turn into something exploitative. They may not see themselves as vulnerable, but those who want to exploit them can. It is this which means that young people who experiment can put themselves at risk to sexual predators, or to people who will take advantage of them. However, as in Andrea's views above, there is a point of contention present within the professionals' accounts. Andrea's concerns that young people have a distorted view of those who exploit young people as being "paedophiles as being dirty old men in macs who go after very young children" is one also shared, as noted elsewhere in this chapter, by the professionals themselves. This view is also one represented within policy. It is *children* who are emphasised as being 'at risk' from '*adult* perpetrators', not young people and not those who may be at risk from other young people.

"It's 'I'll do what I want'": teenage rebelliousness and naivety

Concerns about young people's emerging sense of agency featured within a number of accounts. They spoke of young people who were "beginning to develop a sense of independence" and who are "testing boundaries" in negative ways:

> **Dave (fostering):** I work in foster care and watch children running away and being found in houses [pause] it's 'I'll do what I want', it's that rebelliousness within adolescence that they think they know better, um, but are actually quite vulnerable, but are not prepared to listen to adults, to tell them otherwise, so I think it can be a lot of things, I think the younger children? *no,* because they haven't the maturity to understand, I think with teenagers they're going through *so* many changes, that they feel they know what's best they can do what they want and they'll rebel, and they think on one hand they're being treated as an adult, but actually they're being abused, but they latch on to that

The professionals spoke of how young people are "unwise to the ways of the world". There was the understanding that young people engage in risky behaviours, and are vulnerable to sexual exploitation because of their rebelliousness, their undeveloped sense of awareness and lack of emotional intelligence. Informing many of the professionals' accounts was an assumption of 'essential characteristics in young people because of their age' such as ignorance and rebellion, and an 'assumed link between physical growth and social identity' (Wyn and White, 1997: 12). As Dave observes above, young people can rebel, and not listen to the protective adults around them. It is this which makes young people at risk to abusive adults; abusive adults who treat them as adults, not as the young people they are. As Luke explains:

> **Luke (alternative education):** they may enjoy the sex side of it, the attention and the gifts and the um, you know I guess they would value that. And that's where the exploitation comes in you know, they're childlike, they're a child in their brain and development and that is being exploited by someone who um, perhaps has an awareness that um you know that they are not fully developed as an adult as a person who um would perhaps be able to make a valid decision about whether it is a good thing or not

Luke, as did other participants, displayed normative understandings of youth as a stage of transition, drawing particularly on the 'childhood' aspects of 'youth' to explain why some young people may be sexually exploited. Young people were not always talked about as (fully) agentic subjects, with authenticity attributed to their actions; and it was young people's 'childlikeness', their emotional naivety, their lack of ability to give any kind of informed consent, that was deemed as putting them at risk of being exploited for sex. Thus young people's 'emerging agency' was typically understood to be problematic because young people were seen as seeking adulthood before they were ready to cope with it:

> **Jack (youth justice):** this whole [pause] *rush* into adulthood, in terms of if you drink and you smoke and you're having sex, if you're taking drugs, these are the things that adults do, therefore I'll do them you know, and I think that's, that's part of it isn't it, that's part of the process, the need to be older than you are, to be seen to be older than you are

Many professionals talked of concerns about young people who were not engaged in (what they considered to be) positive activities, so they were without responsibility or structure to guide them. They spoke of young people who were "party party", and "looking to enjoy themselves", and of young people taking drugs and alcohol because it was "exciting", "fun" and because they had "nothing else to do".

Youth as a risk?

While the professionals did invoke specific indicators of risk or 'risky behaviours', they tended to speak in more general terms of young people's risk from sexual exploitation. Young people were talked about as 'at risk' primarily *because they are young people*. Underpinning the ways the professionals made sense of young people's risk to sexual exploitation were normative (partial) assumptions of youth as an inherently 'risky' period of transition spliced with conceptions of childhood as a time of (primarily sexual) innocence. 'Young people' were conceptualised by the professionals as leaving behind a time of innocence, asexuality and 'unworldly naivety' (Faulkner 2011: 78) and entering an inherently risky phase of youth. One in which they understood there to be a potential threat of an emerging agency and sexuality; a phase in which young people 'naturally' rebel and sexually experiment; at a time when 'hormones' mean that they may become overly 'sexualised', not act responsibly and rationally, and when they are without the psychological awareness to realise or understand risk; it is 'as if adolescence were a period of 'meltdown' – a crucial phase where the once "solid" child is recast, via a period of flux, into a new adult "solid"' (Marshall and Stenner, 2004: 18). It is, then, a period that provokes both anxiety and suspicion (Hall and Montgomery, 2000) and bound within the professionals' talk about risk were concerns about young people who are outside of positive adult influences, protection and supervision. For example, the professionals spoke of their concerns about young people who "hang out on the street" and "go missing", and of young people who are "out of the mainstream", "streetwise" and "hard to reach". Within this fraught time of youth, young people are in need of protection, guidance and supervision:

> **Martin (education):** once the hormones kick in at puberty then we know that [pause] they are still children who are, going through the transition into adulthood [pause] usually there is a period of people *becoming* adults, I feel that during that period, while they are still children,

there is a protection that we need to have within a culture,
as they are struggling to become the adults that they are
supposed to be

Similarly to the young people, the professionals actively sought to
avoid providing a pathological or causal explanation for a young
person's involvement in sexual exploitation. So while the professionals
talked primarily of their concerns about young people in care, not
in school and of those who may be perceived by society as 'difficult',
they also insisted that it was important not to 'stereotype', and spoke
of how sexual exploitation could happen to any *young person*. As Linda
explains, sexual exploitation can occur to anyone who is emotionally
vulnerable: all young people are emotionally vulnerable by nature of
their youth, thus all young people are *at risk* to those who want to
exploit or harm them:

> **Linda (community work):** It could happen to anyone, I
> mean that's the problem you know, I think [pause] anyone
> who is emotionally vulnerable so that could be anyone
> and that's for all *social areas or classes*, anyone, um, and
> teenagers are, um [pause] a sort of wry definition of being
> an adolescent is that they are all emotionally vulnerable
> and if someone wants to harm that emotional vulnerability
> then they can

Yet when risk is conceptualised in this way, the individual young person
becomes somewhat lost. It is as if young people are empty vessels with
an undeveloped 'self' waiting to emerge, easily directed and influenced
by their surroundings (see Wyn and White, 1997). There is little room
within this construction to appreciate the nature of young people's
agency, or the underlying common sense rationalities behind young
people's engagement in 'risky' activities. Moreover, positioning young
people in this way arguably ignores young people's circumstances
and realities (O'Connell Davidson, 2005). Instead of 'childhoods' –
influenced and constitutive of the psycho-social dynamics of young
people's own agency, race, class, gender, and place – there is instead
an invocation of a universal 'childhood', and phase of 'youth' (Heinze,
2000). Informing the views of all the professionals, sometimes overtly
so, sometimes not, but always *there* and at work, is the category of
'young people', deployed not only as a descriptive label but also an
explanatory one. The category is homogenous and its explanatory
power derives from and depends on it being so; young people are all

alike *as* young people, in that they are predisposed to behave as they do because they are, at times, irrational, rebellious, hormonal and without maturity. These imputed characteristics may be cast as regrettable, they may be something to cause concern, worry and despair among adults who are responsible for young people, but they are perceived as immutable, not something to be escaped from; they are what it is to be a young person – any young person. A shared dictum therefore was that young people who are less visible to the gaze of protective adults are understood to be 'at risk' because, by nature of their youth, they can become visible and accessible to those who wish to exploit them.

This shared assumption marks out a fundamental difference between what professionals and the young people had to say about sexual exploitation and why it happens; in particular, what each of these groups had to say about risk. The professionals spoke of how sexual exploitation could happen to any *young person*, because to do 'risky things' is tied up somehow with what it is to be young. Thus to rebel, to be irrational, to experiment sexually, to drink, to take drugs and to 'hang out', out of sight and away from responsible adults is a consequence of being young. Young people are at risk of being sexually exploited because it is in doing such 'risky things' that they become visible targets to those who wish to exploit them; and they are easily exploited for sex because they are young people, and hold such characteristics of what it is to be young.

This was not so for the young people, who instead spoke of how sexual exploitation is something that could happen to any*one*, any person. That is to say, the young people did not offer up, or seem to call upon, some normative notion of what it is to be young to explain how it is that they themselves and others might find themselves in sexually exploitative situations and relationships. Any reference to their youth was made typically in relation to a taken-for-granted assumption of adult authority over them because of their age. They considered 'sexual exploitation' to be something that is preventable, something that could happen to anyone if they too experienced such a lack of support, concern, acknowledgement and lack of care that the young people claimed they had experienced. They talked about risk but did not talk about *being young* as being itself 'risky'. Instead, risk was conceptualised by the young people as the adversity they faced and their ways of coping with it. As argued in Chapter Two, they experienced many factors in their lives as blotting out their individuality and subjectivity. They felt themselves to be excluded, different, ignored. Moreover, they spoke of feeling unnoticed and invisible to significant others while simultaneously perceived as objects of surveillance and of concern, rather than as active subjects. Sex, alcohol, drugs and 'hanging out' with peers can be understood as symbolic gestures of resistance and attempts by the young people to assert themselves as individuals. These 'risky behaviours' were spoken of by young people as understandable, albeit self-destructive, ways of coping by not coping at all. Yet, from the view of the professionals, a young person is primarily at risk *because they are young*. Thus the professionals arguably 'do' what the young people speak of: in conceptualising young people in this way, their individualism and their agency remains unacknowledged and rendered invisible.

Yet perhaps necessarily so. While the young people were making sense of their personal experiences, the professionals were making sense of child sexual exploitation, and how young people come to be sexually exploited, within a discursive framework that conceptualises this issue in a particular way. As I have argued previously, it is one in which 'grooming' dominates, and in which young people are positioned as passive objects, thus negating the idea that a young person might exercise agency, and which does not encourage or allow space for the professionals to consider young people's involvement in sexual exploitation outside of coercion or manipulation from some adult abuser (Melrose, 2012). Set within this context, the professionals' talk about risk can *also* be considered to be reflective of how they make sense of and reconcile the challenges presented by the young people they work with, who they perceive as being determined to place themselves at risk, with their understandings of sexual exploitation. As can be seen below, within all the professionals' accounts were references to young people's active choices to place themselves in sexually exploitative situations:

> **Max (children's residential care):** the kids carry on nonetheless, I know what I'm doing, but I'm going to do it anyway, um, they are very difficult to deal with, *very* difficult

> **Nick (social work):** it was something the staff found really *difficult* to deal with, *because* she was going of her own free will, and they didn't have many powers to stop her

> **Louisa (social work):** they were vulnerable but they were making a choice to leave where it was safe and go and meet these men

Jack (youth justice): young people are to a certain extent complicit in the pattern of behaviour

Cathy (fostering): she had wilfully gone out, with the police as her only means to get home

When the concept of grooming features so strongly within the professionals' own accounts, and is supported within public and more formal policy and practice discourses, the young people they spoke of who appear to put themselves at risk present something of a contradiction. They are not *easily* accounted for. Yet they *were* accounted for, in that the professionals spoke of them as being 'at risk' and as being sexually exploited. Hence when they spoke of how a young person appears to be "complicit" or "wilful", with the knowledge of what they are doing, making choices to leave where they are (presumed) safe, and going of their own "free will" to these sexually exploitative situations and relationships, it is because they are being irrational, rebellious, hormonal and without maturity. The circularity of the discourse can make sense of any contradictory element because putting yourself at risk from those who sexually exploit is intimately bound up in what it is to be young. Hence, it was argued by professionals that young people's assertions of agency and consent in relation to a sexually exploitative relationship were a result of 'normal' expressions of youthful challenging behaviour.

Young people's agency presents challenges in other ways too. What is also notable across the professionals' accounts is a sense of unease in talking openly about young people's risk and involvement in sexual exploitation, and a desire to circumvent any impression that a young person may be consenting or choosing in any way to put themselves at risk. There was an implicit, sometimes explicit, acknowledgement that 'choices' made by young people could be associated with blame and just desserts in the minds of some – a point that Louisa sought to distance herself from:

Louisa (social work): they needed to be *empowered*, to make the *right* decision and to protect *themselves*, and *not* keep putting themselves in that position. And that's, not uh in *no way* am I saying that it's their fault for what happened or *blaming them*

The professionals are also arguably demonstrating an awareness of normative understandings of risk and responsibility in which risk is conceptualised as a moral issue. Self-discipline and responsibility are central to the neoliberal discourse surrounding citizenship in which certain behaviours are permissible but others are not. As I noted in Chapter One, to take certain risks can be blameworthy and thereby to appear to actively pursue risk is to be responsible and held accountable for one's actions (Smith et al, 2007). Indeed, a number of professionals were aware that to acknowledge a young person's agency could be to somehow suggest the young person is responsible for putting themselves at risk, and hence to imply that the young person is somehow *not* being sexually exploited or a victim of sexual exploitation. The passage below is notable because it highlights the moral ambiguities within the occupational imagination and furthermore stands as a rare occasion where an interpretation of young people's agency, consent or choices were not explained by reference to their youth:

Annette (third sector): because she was inviting them into the flat they weren't forcing their way into the flat, they were invited *in*, and if they were ever asked to leave they left, so they weren't actually doing anything

Sophie: Right, I see, so uh in your mind uh, what would you, what did you think about that situation

Annette: Hmmm, I don't uh that. *That* [pause] I struggled with, because I I'm not *sure, that I would ever say*, that I was ever able to say that these *weren't choices* that she was making because she was given, lots of support, *lots of* opportunities, to [pause] *to turn it around*, or stop it or and it it *clearly* she was being *clearly* she was a victim but I [pause] it it's difficult isn't it I mean that sort of victim thing is quite an *emotive* thing, and yes *of course* she was a victim, but I think her being a *victim* started an awful lot, *further away*, than that particular situation, I think *then,* I'm not sure maybe that she really *was* a victim because, I think that she was using it herself I think that she was using it to get what *she* wanted, she *knew* what she was doing, but she didn't *know* what she was doing, and from *that* in that respect, I think you know we very clearly got to the point, where there was *very* little more that we could do, because she *knew* exactly what she was doing and she was making the choice to do it [pause] um and I think she she was a victim of circumstances right probably from being a little girl she was, you know had led her to that point

The dilemma that Annette illuminates is to acknowledge the young person as both active agent and victim of sexual exploitation. It as if there is some tacit assumption that sexual exploitation and the young person's choices must be considered in isolation from each other, and it is this which Annette struggles to do. It was clear to Annette, that the young person "knew exactly what she was doing, and she was making the choice to do it". Yet, Annette still considered her to be a victim of sexual exploitation because the choices the young person was understood to be making were related to the young person's history and circumstances. Annette's hesitancy suggests a concern that to impute choice is to deny victim status. The professionals' talk about risk can also be seen as illustrative of the limitations of the discursive framework of 'child sexual exploitation'. As Biggs (2001: 304–5) argues,

> policies not only respond to social ills, they also consecrate them. They contribute to the constellation of ideas and evidence that create the problem itself ... through the agency of social policy formation, certain issues are legitimised. They are shaped and made visible in particular ways.

As discussed throughout, grooming has become a dominant discourse for explaining and understanding child sexual exploitation thus obscuring other possible reasons and routes into the exchange of sex (Melrose, 2012). In so doing, young people's subjective capacity for agency and choice is obscured, as are their individual needs, circumstances and social conditions. Within this dominant discourse there is little encouragement or space for professionals to consider young people's expressions of consent, their agency and the circumstances underpinning their involvement in sexual exploitation (Phoenix, 2002). The young person who is seen to put themselves at risk must have a reason for doing so if they are to fit within an understanding of sexual exploitation.

This aspect was something many of the professionals seemed not unaware of. They talked of difficulties with getting colleagues to recognise young people as being sexually exploited. They spoke of how people think young people 'are going out there asking for it', and the importance of 'getting people to see that it's not a conscious choice for these young people'. An example of this is given by Andrea:

Andrea (healthcare): sexual exploitation and sexual offences are *really really really difficult cases*, to get through the Crown Prosecution Service [pause] and they have I think the Crown Prosecution Service are not [pause] they haven't got their heads around the sexual exploitation crimes, unless they have groups of people involved, um, or if there is grooming of younger children. So again, in that group where it's the 15-year-old, who is below the age of consent *but who can probably consent because that's their boyfriend and that's alright isn't it*. And if there's lots of professionals from different areas saying no it's not normal at all, because X Y Z then they might listen, but I think there's that feeling of this kind of *no man's land*. Vulnerable young people who police recognise as vulnerable but every time they process, something as an offence, and it's not going anywhere, and *yet* it's going to happen *again*

As discussed previously, within normative conceptions of youth and childhood, young people are the interstitial category; they are part child, part adult. Children we worry about, adults we leave to themselves; it is 'young people' who *give* us cause to worry. They can be responsible and blameless, 'at risk' and 'a risk', 'trouble' or 'in trouble'. 'Young people' are understood to sit in 'a no man's land', to use Andrea's phrase, because they can be perceived by others as being able to look after themselves and, thus, both their responsibility and their vulnerability – and by extension their sexual exploitation – can be called into question. Andrea goes on to explain how:

Andrea (healthcare): sometimes young people are very plausible and are more articulate and I've seen this in [pause] in other people's assessments when I've read other workers assessments and what's been said, even very young children, so and so is intelligent and articulate. So does that make them all of a sudden not sexually exploited? But there is that um, *oh well if they can speak like that and talk like that then they must be fine* they must be able to look after themselves

Andrea's concern is that it is perceptions of a child or young person's maturity, their perceived ability to look after themselves, which can influence whether they are assessed as being sexually exploited, or not. For young people to be *deserving* victims they must be passive and not active subjects (see also Montgomery, 1998). Some participants spoke in a similar way about their concerns for the way boys at risk can be perceived:

> **Sandra (education):** the young men that probably need,
> I would expect *need help*, from sexual exploitation are
> probably in the custody suites, they are probably seen already
> as *offenders* rather than victims

Such concerns are echoed elsewhere whereby boys are more likely to be seen as offenders than in need of support (see for example McMullen, 1987; Davies and Feldman, 1992; Palmer, 2001). There is something of a shared assumption that it is not enough for young people to *be* children (that is, as a social category defined within the CSE policy framework and the United Nations Convention on the Rights of the Child), they must be *like* children. Ideally, they should evince those characteristics often associated with childhood – innocent, sexually unknowing, undeveloped and in need of protection (see Piper, 2000). We glimpse this within Andrea and Sandra's reflections above. Young people's vulnerability and official acknowledgement of their sexual exploitation can be called into question if they are seen as intelligent, articulate, knowledgeable and responsible. Thus, emphasising a young person's childlikeness can become occupationally necessary in order to claim some authentic status of vulnerable victim when they engage in risky activities and practices:

> **Mary (healthcare):** I've had a sexual exploitation referral,
> and I've said *the reason why I am so concerned* is that this *child*
> and I try and use the word child as much as possible so
> it reminds us all that yes this is a child not just a stroppy
> teenager who is 5 inches taller than me, *this child* is now
> having anal sex as a method of contraception [pause] This.
> Is. What. I am worried about, and then everyone will go,
> *ugh,* oh oh really

As Mary explains, it was not enough for her to describe the circumstances the young person was in, but she also considered it necessary to emphasise and invoke the concept of 'child' in order to seek a response from other colleagues. The passage below in which Marie refers to adult women reinforces this point further:

> **Marie (third sector):** it was reinforcing that the women
> that we are working with, emotionally they are probably

> only 5 or 6 years old, they are so so damaged, and so you
> can talk chronological age as much as you want but then
> you have to balance that with emotional ability, like my
> daughter when she was 14 she was probably far more *stable*
> than an 18-, 19-, 35- year-old that we see out working on
> the streets

'Chronological age' is of limited relevance because the women Marie
works with are *like* children. They are emotionally damaged and so
are childlike in their emotional ability. In fact, as Marie explains,
some of these women can be *more* like children than actual children.
It is their childlike status which must be reinforced rather than their
circumstances, social conditions or the sexually exploitative situations
they are in. It is because they are *like* children that we are invited to
understand that they are still vulnerable.

Agency

The above exploration reveals something of the difficulties those
working with young people face, in accommodating an understanding
of risk and 'risky behaviours' held by the young people and considered
earlier, within a contemporary framing of child sexual exploitation (or
indeed an historical one). As I outlined in Chapter One, it has been
assumptions about consent, choice and responsibility which have been
central to the historical and contemporary framing of this issue, and
which have seen children and young people deemed and treated as
offenders (see also Brown, 2004). Historically, the depiction of children
and young people involved in the exchange of sex has been as innocent
victims of an adult other, or as blameworthy deviants responsible
for their actions (Ennew, 1986; Brown 2004). This culminated in a
binary depiction of young people involved in prostitution with the
introduction of legislation at the turn of the 20th century to reconfigure
the issue to one of social care and not criminal justice. This binary
representation of the agentic offender and powerless victim has been
removed in current UK and Welsh Government policy (see WAG,
2011) by stating that the grooming process employed by perpetrators
means that 'no child can give informed consent' (see for example
WAG, 2011: 9). This position on young people's agency is reinforced
and affirmed through campaign literature, such as that produced by
the National Working Group for Child Sexual Exploitation, and it
can be seen in Casey's (2015) report to the UK government, in which
she reinforces this positioning of children and young people by stating

that there are no circumstances in which children can consent, or be seen to be making choices (Casey, 2015: 3). While both have always been present, we have swung from a dominant mythical depiction of a predatory, wilful, deviant young offender, to the depiction of the powerless, dependent victim who is at risk from the (adult) predatory deviant male.

Set in this context, as I have already indicated in the previous chapter, it is not the wider issues surrounding sexual exploitation or the exchange of sex that underpin CSE policy discourse. It is not that children and young people are politically, socially and economically more vulnerable (O'Connell Davidson, 2005), nor is it understandings of agency, or wider conditions of consent that tax policy (see Pitts, 1997; Pearce, 2009; 2013) – unless it is to claim that no consent of any form can be given. As Moore (2006: 79–82) rather forcefully argues, the grooming discourse can be seen as an 'essentialist feminised victim philosophy that robbed children of their agency and thus any criminal responsibility'. It is grooming which forms the sole reason for and why children and young people become involved in and abused through exchanging sex for something.

However, this also, at some level, cements the paradoxical status of a child or young person involved in the exchange of sex. The problem of the normative rational citizen – the problem of choice, risk, and responsibility – still exists. While it is important to recognise that the emphasis on children and young people's innocence has been a necessary challenge to previous traditions of blame against victims of sexual abuse, it must also be acknowledged that the emphasis on the assumed innate innocence of children is problematic for children and young people who are not so readily perceived as dependent, passive and weak. They can be seen as 'non-children', non-defensible and not so deserving of protection (see Kitzinger, 2006: 168–9). In this way, the boundaries of child sexual exploitation mean that a young person's vulnerability, risk and, to some extent, their sexual exploitation depends on their fitting within normative conceptions of what it is to be a child and what it is to be 'groomed'. In this particular framework of understanding, there is no way of accommodating the young people's framing of risk and why or how it is that young people may come to be sexually exploited.

The current framing and discourse surrounding child sexual exploitation is problematic in another way too. As Coy (2016: 5) suggests, 'the suppression of young people's sense of agency is both cause and consequence of separating CSE from prostitution'. When the distinction between sex work and sexual exploitation rests on a denial of child or young people's agency, and their psychological inability to consent, rather than conditions of consent, their own feelings of agency and/or their entitlement to and need of support, we lose the opportunity to understand the symbolic meaning of young people's actions and how and when they assert their agency (or not). The ways young people mark boundaries, articulate identity and difference become lost in binary representations of young people as victim or culprit (Hebdige, 1988). The discursive formation of 'sexual exploitation' necessarily positions young people as object and passive, and means that young people cannot be spoken of as active agents (Melrose, 2012). When a child or young person exerts agency, and does not act like a 'proper victim' – when they appear to wilfully put themselves at risk, when they reject offers of help, when they are young offenders themselves – their status as victims of sexual exploitation can be questioned (Williams, 2010; Phoenix, 2010), or go unnoticed – which is a point I return to in the next chapter. As we have seen intimated in the professionals' narratives, fundamentally, there is a lack of discursive capacity or conceptual insights to make sense of and explain young people's risk in the same ways that the young people did when the boundaries of this problem are so intrinsically linked to (partial) conceptions of childhood in order to legitimise the very problem itself. If we are to fully apprehend and understand the aetiology of sexual exploitation, young people's agency and more nuanced understandings of risk must be made visible.

As argued earlier, child sexual exploitation as constructed within policy and practice has become unhelpfully simplified to a problem of 'men who exploit', and the consequent need for protection/control of individual children, rather than a problem constructed around the social conditions and problems that children and young people face (Phoenix, 2002: 359). This leaves little space to understand young people's sense of and expressions of agency, their own meanings of consent, or to understand risk taking as anything other than normal youthful behaviours (if one is outside of positive adult influences). So while the young people's narratives do to some extent seem to 'fit' with established risk indicators within policy and practice, in grasping the salience of these indicators it is important to understand how individual young people themselves perceive risk and their sense of agency, and the inter-relationship of both in understanding their actions (see also O'Connell Davidson, 2005; Pearce, 2009; Phoenix, 2010; Melrose, 2010). What may appear to be 'risk taking' may be young people's situational responses to complex circumstances. What may *appear* to be illogical may not be so when set within a framework of understanding that positions these behaviours as ways of coping (see Wyn and White, 1997).

In this sense, the young people's engagement in 'risky behaviours' could be considered as a form of symbolic resistance to their perceived circumstances of isolation and neglect (Hebdige, 1988). Or 'experienced as an assertion of the self as subject, not as being transformed into an object' (O'Connell Davidson 2005: 55). By making themselves 'unseen' either physically or metaphorically, they protected themselves from their feelings of being unwanted and ignored. Drugs and alcohol were a way the young people could prove to themselves that they did 'exist' and offered a way for the young people to feel they were in control and powerful, or at the very least forget feelings of constrained agency and powerlessness. In their talk about drugs and alcohol, they were able to feel hidden away 'inside' and, in trying to mask the way they felt inside, they were also able to feel 'out' and in control. Alcohol thus provided the opportunity of coping by enabling them to 'obliterate' themselves and disappear, while also having a way of 'being in and seeing the world' (Willis, 1990: 108). Sex too was considered to be a way of dealing with how they felt and a way of asserting or feeling a sense of agency where they may have felt as object – with young people's involvement in negative sexual encounters as a perverse means of regaining ownership over their bodies (see for example O'Neill, 2001; Pearce et al, 2002; Moore, 2006; Clutton and Coles, 2007). 'Sleeping around' and getting paid for sex can be understood as an embodied symbolic gesture towards an assertion of the self. It can be seen as 'throwing your self away before they do it for you' (Hebdige, 1988: 32). This is also a reminder that young people's risky behaviours, and their sexual exploitation, can only be understood in the context of their everyday lives and circumstances – those 'things going on' that the young people in this study explained as the risks that can lead a person to feel vulnerable and seek ways to respond to those feelings of vulnerability and powerlessness.

The professionals interviewed operate broadly within this discourse of sexual exploitation. As discussed, their understandings of risk are arguably informed by and are illustrative of it. Normative understandings of youth, strongly inflected with (partial) conceptions of childhood, underpinned the ways professionals conceptualised *and* legitimised young people's 'risk' to sexual exploitation. They made sense of, justified and reflected on the problems associated with understanding young people's 'risky behaviours' by drawing on prevalent normative categories of youth. While they recognised young people's active agency, they were careful to not attribute blame or responsibility to a young person. Neither was there any kind of moral projection of deviancy on to the general or specific young people they spoke of. In fact, they made efforts to the contrary, to which these conceptions of youth and childhood were central. To reiterate, in order to make sense of and to have others recognise an agentic yet vulnerable and 'at risk' young person, there is the ever present category of youth to invoke. It is homogenising and its *explanatory* and *justificatory* power derives from, and depends on, it being so. While this may secure a perception of children and young people who do not fit within a typical understanding of CSE as victims of abuse, it homogenises young people, and does not allow for an understanding of risk taking behaviour in the ways that the young people in this study spoke of. As discussed in this and the previous chapter, more nuanced understandings of young people's vulnerabilities and risk are needed and young people's agency must be made visible within a discourse of child sexual exploitation in order to fully apprehend both the complexity of their social and emotional worlds and the problem of sexual exploitation itself. It is to the matter of sexual exploitation – what it is, and how it occurs, that the discussion now turns.

FOUR

Exchange and abuse

Exchange (noun): an act of giving one thing and receiving another (especially of the same kind) in return.

Abuse (noun): use (something) to bad effect or for a bad purpose; misuse; treat with cruelty or violence, especially regularly or repeatedly.

(Oxford English Dictionary)

Child sexual exploitation is no longer a 'hidden issue'.[1] As I have noted throughout this book, it is a problem now prominent in public awareness. At the time of writing, high profile criminal trials relating to charges of organised child sexual exploitation in Rochdale, Derby, Oxford and most recently Rotherham have been the focus of significant national media attention, prompting widespread political and public debate, in particular around the 'grooming' of children and young people by gangs of male, predatory adults. A two-year national inquiry instigated by the Children's Commissioner for England reported in late 2013 on the nature and extent of Child Sexual Exploitation in Gangs and Groups, with the inquiry's interim report opening with this grim assessment: '[t]he reality is that each year thousands of children in England are raped and abused from as young as 11 years by people seeking to humiliate, violate and control them and the impact on their lives is often devastating' (Berelowitz et al, 2012: 5). Alongside this attention, investigations into historical cases of child sexual abuse by prominent figures such as Jimmy Savile and Rolf Harris have seen the terms 'child sexual exploitation' and 'child sexual abuse' used interchangeably in media reporting and discussion. In addition, concerns over young people's sexual behaviours and relationships – the uses and abuses of 'sexting' and sexual violence – while not often referred to as sexual exploitation, are brought into debates about CSE over concerns about the absence of (and the desire to promote) 'healthy relationships' among young people.

So what is CSE? Rape? Sexual abuse? Grooming? All those things? As I considered in Chapter One, there is no agreed policy definition of CSE. In the four UK nations, there are, to date, four separate definitions of the problem. Extending out more widely from the UK, there is no globally recognised definition or understanding of sexual exploitation, with references to child prostitution, or the commercial sexual exploitation of children being far more common.[2] Returning to the UK, while the definitions are different, what is common to each nation is a conception of sexual exploitation underpinned by a grooming model (Melrose, 2012; 2013).[3] 'Grooming' has become synonymous with CSE and, arguably, stands as a way of explaining not just how it happens but what the problem is.

In this chapter I want to do two things. First, I explore the different ways that both groups of participants from this study understood sexual exploitation to occur. I consider how 'grooming' may not always feature and, building on previous discussion, for some young people exchanging sex can be a coping response to other difficulties, and a way of feeling as subject (as opposed to object). Second, in considering these different models for understanding CSE, I argue that the element of *exchange* is fundamental to each. I am not the first to raise the issue of exchange. As far back as 1992, Green offered an understanding of child prostitution as children and young people providing 'sexual services *in exchange* for some sort of payment, such as money, drink, drugs, other consumer goods, or even a bed and a roof over one's head for the night' (my emphasis, Green, 1992: 5; see also Calder, 2001). However, I want to extend out from this and suggest that exchange is what makes sexual exploitation particular and distinct from other forms of child sexual abuse. More than this, it is essential to any understanding of CSE, bringing attention to and recognition of unmet needs, agency, and the sorts of object/subject experiences discussed thus far and which I continue to explore in this chapter.

Grooming: 'brainwashing' and coercion

The analysis begins here by introducing those accounts from the young people that might be familiar in that they show a close fit with a grooming model of sexual exploitation, in which there is a predatory adult targeting younger children through the provision of attention or gifts and which results in sexual abuse (see Chapter One). Leah and Claire talked about how they had met people they did not know through the internet and this "ended up" in them "doing things they didn't understand". As Claire tells us:

> **Claire:** they basically, brainwashing you to get you to like them for what they are pretending to be, and you end up

having intimate conversations and end up getting even more intimate and then you end up doing stuff that you don't want to do …. it's easier for the predator to attack young people, because they don't realise they're being brainwashed and with the compliments they are getting they feel more self-esteem and then something bad happens … and making them do things that they didn't really, understand or don't know what's happening and they've got no one to talk to and they just hide themselves away

Claire met her abuser through the internet. He was an older man and pretended to be a young teenager, like Claire. For Claire, the person she met was, in her view, a "predator", pretending to be someone authentically caring in order to "brainwash" and "attack" her by making her feel better about herself, by giving her confidence and raising her self-esteem. There is something evident in the language Claire uses here which appears as an 'exterior vocabulary', as a learned model, which she is drawing on to make sense of her experiences (Hall and Coffey, 2007: 280). Nonetheless, Claire is using it to make sense of her encounters in which there was a *process* whereby someone had artfully gained her trust and exploited this. Claire did not recognise the grooming techniques or the true age or motives of the person concerned until too late. Her experience is represented prominently in the current discourse of CSE, and can be seen almost mirrored in the current definition of sexual exploitation in Wales, '[t]he vulnerability of the young person and grooming process employed by perpetrators renders them powerless to recognise the exploitative nature of relationships and unable to give informed consent' (WAG, 2011: 9). Claire and Leah's accounts also align closely with practice literature on grooming which outlines that an adult sex abuser 'cultivates' the young (depicted as primarily female) person's vulnerability – 'her low self-esteem, her feeling of helplessness and her need for love and protection' (van Meeuwen et al, 1998). Their accounts also share similarities with what the adult participants had to say about how young people can be sexually exploited. A prominent theme across all the professionals' accounts was the notion of 'grooming', or some reference or language which implied their adherence to a grooming model of child sexual exploitation. They spoke of how young people – typically girls – were at risk of being 'sucked in' and 'groomed' by adult men who were looking to take advantage of their vulnerability. Carla's explanation is typical of these sorts of accounts and aligns closely with those given by Claire and Leah:

> **Carla (children's residential care):** when a *man* or
> whatever well cos it's mainly the girls really isn't it but he
> says oh I love you, that's all he's got to say even if he don't
> mean it, and he just wants to take advantage but if he says
> that and shows a bit gives her a cuddle or *something* warm
> which is something they haven't had for goodness knows
> *how long* from their families, that they're sucked in straight
> away, and they'll do anything then for that person

Young people were understood to be at risk because they are
'brainwashed', 'manipulated' and unable to see the calculated intent
behind the emotional warmth that is being given. Others spoke
of grooming in a way that is more suggestive of the 'sophisticated
grooming and priming processes executed by abusing adults' considered
by Clutton and Coles (2007: 8). Participants spoke of clever, systematic,
targeted exploitation in which single men or groups of men employ
a number of grooming techniques over a period of time. This is
summarised well by Andrea:

> **Andrea (healthcare):** there were things like from being
> really nice and paying my phone contract to, I'm only
> allowed to use my phone when he's got access because he
> pays for my phone, I'm only allowed to use it when he
> can see who I've called and read my texts, so you get those
> controlling things, and then, the last thing was he then
> introduced her to friends, so he was now *ready to share her*

'Grooming' itself was talked of as "giving young people some of the
good stuff" – such as affection, attention, security, money, drink, and
drugs – while employing a gradual increase in control in order to use
the young person for sex.

However, we can see in Claire's account, rather than, simplistically,
the predator 'cultivating' her, she became of notice to someone, and
felt acknowledged as a person through the relationship and intimacy
that obtained (see also Sennett, 2003). The vital care and attention
she was missing from those around her who *should* provide this was
given to her by the predator, and it is *this* which made 'grooming' her
possible. That she had no one to talk to when things went "bad" is a
reminder of Claire's pronouncement heard in Chapter Two that she was
not acknowledged by others. It was because of her lack of recognition
from family and carers that she was talking to people on the internet
– putting her in the way of "the predator". Yet also, and importantly

for Claire, it was this lack of recognition and acknowledgement which made her vulnerable to the person who sexually exploited her. These accounts from the young people suggest that to fully understand grooming as a form of sexual exploitation, consideration must also be given to the wider context of a young person's relationships and circumstances (see Phoenix, 2002).

This point is evident from the professionals account too, but in a different way. Many of the professionals spoke of young people coming into contact with people through their families – people they could be closely connected to but whom they did not know intimately: such as friends of friends, family acquaintances, neighbours' friends, step-family members. These family connections were understood to make young people *accessible* to exploiting males, while also giving *legitimacy* to these sexually exploitative relationships. This point, while acknowledged within literature relating to child sexual abuse, and indicated within Welsh Government guidance (see WAG, 2011:14), is interestingly not much developed within the literature on sexual exploitation (see Kelly et al, 1995). The prominent understanding is of an adult 'other', while there is a tendency to frame CSE as occurring outside of and away from the family. A point to note is that young people can know their abusers, their abusers can be family members, and/or their families can be aware of the exploitation.

While the grooming model provides *a* way of understanding the encounters and experiences of some participants, it was not the *only* way the participants accounted for sexual exploitation, as the chapter now reveals.

Transactional sex: 'conditions and rewards', 'bad relationships'

All the young people talked of their experiences as occurring through 'bad relationships'. These relationships were those in which the young people considered themselves as 'partners', 'boyfriends' or 'girlfriends' or 'going out with' the person in question. The relationships were considered to be 'bad' because of their conditional character, about which the young people spoke of 'pressure' to 'have to do things':

> **Katie:** it's different for different people isn't it? Like my story. They say they love you. They buy you things. And then once you're under the thumb you're fucked. They say oh I do these things for you and you have to do things for them. Otherwise they might leave.

> ... He looked after me. He gave me everything.
> Everything I didn't have you know. I was safe there. When
> he knew that he changed. He was like oh come on now
> you've got to start pulling your weight, you know help
> him out.

As Katie explains, sex was a condition of the relationship, and exchanging sex with this boyfriend to 'help him out' was her expected contribution. In many ways Katie's story is similar to the experience of grooming discussed above, and finds some congruence with the policy guidance which states '[t]he perpetrator always holds some kind of power over the young person, increasing the dependence of the victim as the exploitative relationship develops (WAG, 2011: 13). As Katie bluntly explains: "they say they love you ... they buy you things ... and then once you're under the thumb you're fucked". Katie's boyfriend was someone who made her feel safe. He was someone who gave her the care and attention she didn't have from others, and this made her dependent on him. Katie also explained how this dependency was increased when he supplied her with drugs for her drug addiction. Many of the young people's accounts also contained this similar sense of feeling coerced to have to exchange sex or to take part in sexual activities, either with their partners or on their behalf – "to pull their weight" or "help them out".

However, there are some important aspects of the young people's experiences which cannot be accounted for solely within the formal definitions offered in regard to the grooming model. While participants described manipulation and control within their relationships they did not describe being "brainwashed" in the way that, for example, Claire spoke of above. Not all the young people's narratives invoked the notion of being 'powerless to recognise the exploitative nature of relationships' (WAG, 2011: 9). They talked about being aware they were the objects of abusive and manipulative activities, but they explained that there were sufficient reasons why they remained in such relationships. It is important to note that they were not 'blinded' within these relationships or unaware of the motives of others (Phoenix, 2002). Yet leaving the relationship presented them with few and sometimes grim alternatives. These relationships went some way in their feeling safer, wanted, acknowledged and more secure. Consequently, the young people exchanged sex because otherwise, as Katie explained, the person "might leave". Katie goes on to explain how later she remained in the relationship solely because of her need for drugs, and it was only when her addiction (for a time) was under control that she was able to leave the relationship.

There are similarities within such rationales with Williams' (1999: 20) idea of 'transactional sex', defined as 'sex with one person, consistently, in exchange for economic or 'in-kind' support'. As O'Connell Davidson (2005: 56–7) is careful to note, transactional sex is not *necessarily* exploitative and there are 'no firm boundaries between sex for economic gain or personal advantage, and sex for its own sake (or for love or duty)'. That said, the concept of 'transactional sex' here, particularly if understood in an abusive context, provides a useful way of understanding the young people's descriptions of events in that these relationships were meeting some of their needs, and they were recognised as subjects in *some* way within them. It was because of this that the young people accepted the conditions put on them. Sex, and the expectation to perform certain sexual acts, was understood by some of the young people to be a condition 'worth' accepting. This can be seen in the following from Nathan, talking about his experiences in relation to sexuality:

> **Nathan:** … it's really *really* difficult to know how to describe it because um, because of the lack of choice and thing, with um especially if you're closeted because um, it's very hard to start up a conversation with a person with the same type of orientation and. It's, it kind of leads you into accepting things [pause] which you wouldn't normally if there was more people because [pause] you're alone because you've got a secret and you can't tell people about it [pause] so whoever comes along and is able to deal with it whether that be a person who is just going to use you, the fact that you can tell them and you can speak to them [pause] that uh kind of leads you open to [long pause] because it relieves one kind of *strain* on you and you they've got that little bit of control over you, which means they can *twist things* and it can go downhill

Like Claire and Katie, Nathan is describing how he became of notice to someone. He further explains how being able to share his secret about his sexuality enabled him to share *who he really was*. He went from being 'closeted' – in which aspects of his identity were hidden – to being open and visible to another. Drawing on Sennett's work (2003: 117–18), Nathan became visible to someone but in so doing he also became exposed to exploitative consequences. He lost control over when and how he became visible, and the person *in on the secret* had control over him by threatening to expose him and make him feel ashamed. Yet as Nathan explains, it was important for him to share his feelings, to make his sexuality a reality, and to not feel alone. In doing so he was prepared to accept being 'used' because the relationship was, in some way, meeting a need to feel recognised and acknowledged.

The young people's experiences within these "bad" sexually exploitative relationships can be understood in regard to a complex relationship between a young person's common sense understandings of their own social world, their sense of agency, and being treated as both subject and object. Of having more emotional needs met while at the same time being engaged in more objectified exchanges of sex. For example, Nathan talked about "repeating a cycle of being used" because it is "what you know". The young people didn't leave the relationships when these became "twisted" or went "downhill", because, as Sarah explained poignantly, it was "an uncomfortable comfortableness": the young people already considered themselves to be ignored, different, and without support. These bad relationships mirrored and perpetuated these feelings, yet also provided *some* perceived form of security.

The professionals also talked of sexual exploitation in a similar way to the young people's accounts of 'bad relationships'. They spoke of sexual exploitation as occurring through "dodgy", "unhealthy", and "dysfunctional" relationships: relationships deemed to be exploitative because they are controlling, manipulative and abusive, but which are also meeting some of the young person's needs. Faye's comments below bear striking similarities to some of the young people's accounts:

> **Faye (third sector):** some of them were just really plain scared uh, that maybe some of the guys they were with, or boyfriends were incredibly violent and they didn't know what else to do so maybe they got into the drugs, and they, somebody had come up to them and been like *oh* I'll help you and then been uh acted really friendly to them, and they thought they were great and they would look out for them and suddenly, when they didn't even realise *how* it had turned into this really whole twisted thing where, they were working and giving them the money and actually the guy was going to kill them, and they'd cut off everything with their family and they didn't have anywhere else to go, so it was somehow better to be with *somebody* [pause] even though you knew what they were going to do to you [pause] somebody who, well what else could you do

Typical of other professionals' accounts, Faye speaks in a way that is congruent with elements of the policy discourse of sexual exploitation, in that these speak of young people's manipulation and coercion into the exchange of sex. However, as with a number of the young people, they did not speak of sexual exploitation in the sense that they believed the young person to be unaware of the exploitative nature of the relationship. They talked of how the exchange of sex within these abusive relationships formed part of a taken for granted aspect in a young person's life (see also O'Neill 2001). They spoke of how there is a combination of 'conditions and rewards' and so to considered that these relationships were meeting some of a young person's needs, albeit in an abusive way. Young people may nevertheless be manipulated and coerced into exchanging sex, but they were understood to be staying in these relationships because it was *a way* of meeting their needs. Yet this aspect of sexually exploitative relationships is barely recognised within policy guidance and practice discourse, or within the public awareness campaigns about sexual exploitation.

To define these experiences as instances of 'transactional sex' may appear clinical and distanced. Yet it provides a way of grasping the young people's experiences that brings sharp focus to the notion of needs being met in exchange for sex and in doing so implicitly acknowledges young people's agency within these exchanges. This is not to suggest that exploitation or abuse was somehow absent (see Montgomery, 1998; O'Connell Davidson, 2005). The young people's accounts clearly indicated that these were controlling, violent, and physically, sexually and emotionally abusive relationships. At the same time, however, these relationships were meeting needs that were not being met elsewhere. The young people explained how these relationships were the least worst option to them at that time, forcing our attention to the wider networks, relationships, circumstances and contexts within which sexual exploitation takes place.

Transient relationships: 'nothing comes for free'

I now discuss those experiences in which the young people described a much more limited sense of their own agency, in which the exchange of sex was talked about as somehow expected or inevitable:

> **Danny:** I've woken up and been in really dangerous situations like been taken down to [place name] and stuff. And then you can't say no can you. Because you've taken

their drink and they just think you're drunk so they do it anyway.

Danny's account was not untypical in that others spoke of exchanging sex as something that was expected. As can be seen in what Danny says above, and evident in other young participants' accounts is 'a troubled sense of ownership over their bodies' (Coy, 2008: 1415) and a feeling of relative powerlessness over their circumstances. Danny explains that she was "taken" places, and has "woken up and been in really dangerous situations" and "can't say no". As with others she depicts a subjectivity bound up in uncertainty, powerlessness, and troubled sense of agency and ability to consent, requiring a necessary 'blotting out' of herself in order to get by (O'Connell Davidson, 2005: 55). Similarly, other young people spoke of "obviously having to do things" as a price to pay for whatever it was they got – something that can be seen in Katie's comments below:

> *Sophie:* ok so it's not about needing a place to stay it's more about the place where you stay?

> **Katie:** oh that too, you know you need somewhere to stay and people put you up but you learn quickly that nothing comes for free

As discussed previously, James (2000) argues that the body is the medium through which people encounter social relations and, as such, it is intimately connected with our subjectivity. The reality for some participants was that their bodies were a currency that they were expected to use in return for *whatever* it was that was given in exchange. The official guidance recognises the nature of power and control within exploitative relationships and the potential for this to deepen as the relationship persists (WAG, 2011: 13). Yet, notably, the accounts provided in this study did not always invoke notions of more durable or 'developed relationships' as in the above guidance. The young people also talked of people they met more fleetingly, "friends of friends", people who were loosely connected to their group, or people in the houses in which they would wake. For example, Danny relayed multiple instances of sexually exploitative exchanges and encounters with people she barely knew or did not consider herself to be in a 'relationship' with, and which arose as a result of having accepted, or in exchange for, alcohol, lifts or food. There is relatively little of the temporal nature of 'grooming' in these accounts but often a more transient series of encounters in which sex was the expected if not unavoidable currency of exchange. This leads to a point raised in Chapter Two. 'Grooming' here has less to do with a relationship (or relationships) between a young person and someone who might sexually exploit them, and far more to do with the wider relationships, social context, practices and norms within which young people live and which can leave them feeling powerless and objectified and unable to give or enact consent.

'Party' lifestyles and peer bullying

This notion of transient relationships is evident in the professionals' accounts too, albeit in a way that connected sexual exploitation to youth culture and practices. The professional participants spoke of young people's entry into sexual exploitation being linked to group membership and parties. They talked of concerns about young people gathering together and the resulting sexually exploitative relationships or exchanges:

> **Matthew (youth work):** There is this sort of, this thing that sort of plays itself out every Friday Saturday night, where, they just sort of get drunk and again, it's sort of concerning now because it's just getting more and more, I don't know why it's kicking off down there again, and the girls go off down there, and then they sort of egg all the boys on, you know shouting, and the girls don't necessarily get involved in the fighting, but certainly they are encouraging it, and that's a big sort of part of it as well, because it's exciting, it's something to do, but then they are all these sort of by-products of it as well, the boys sort of then, they just seem to sleep with everybody, different people will have slept with somebody else and they'll be, who are you with this week and it will be a different person

In a similar way, others talked about young people looking for 'excitement and fun' being invited to parties with or by adult men. This was talked about in a similar way to grooming – only instead of this occurring between individuals, it involves groups of men grooming young people through parties. As Annette explains:

> **Annette (third sector):** That was you know that would be the way *in* you know getting them to come, cannabis,

getting them oh let's have a party and let's all share cannabis,
let's have a party next week and have a bit more cannabis,
let's party next week and have cannabis and alcohol, and
let's have, and let's all be friends together, and then de de
de de de you know.

Sexual exploitation was also conceptualised as a form of sexual bullying
between young people. This shared some similarity to reflections
about grooming and abusive relationships but was distinctive in that
it was talked of as occurring between young people. As with Polly's
account, sexual exploitation was understood to not always occur in
adult/child relationships:

> **Polly (youth work):** I mean it is a form of bullying isn't
> it, amongst the young people, um although I'm just talking
> about between young people and I'm sure there are adults
> that come in and, you know, take advantage of young
> people … but it's negative peer relationships that come
> out of when young people hang around in groups … and
> there is a problem when they are having sex not because
> they want to but because they feel they have to

As with Polly, other participants talked of grooming and of the
coercion, manipulation and control within peer relationships in which
young people may be persuaded to exchange sex, or to undertake sexual
activities. They did not, however, talk of 'gangs' or organised groups
of young people, rather they spoke of concerns about the existence of
this form of sexual bullying among young people *in general*:

> **Matthew (youth work):** *really,* you know, the filming, the
> sort of introducing to friends and sort of things like this,
> you know, it's the thing on phones isn't it now, and they
> just film each other doing, and you *never* want to look at
> a young person's phone you've just got to go, *not interested
> not even going to look at the screen*, you know the last thing I
> want to do is get a glimpse of anything like that

The discourse of sexual exploitation based on grooming does not easily
recognise peer-on-peer sexual exploitation, despite research evidencing
that this occurs, because the emphasis seems placed mainly on 'abusing
adults' or 'older boyfriends' (see also Pearce, 2009; 2013). Current
policy, where peer exploitation is mentioned, refers only to gangs or

organised groups of young people, or young people who 'recruit' their peers for fear of their own exploitation (see WAG, 2011: 13–14). Yet relationships with peers as well as with adults will inevitably shape understandings of sex, consent and expectations of sex (see Firmin, 2011; also Pearce, 2013).

Exchanging sex to meet needs: Sex work and 'pimping'

I now consider those accounts that intimate notions of choice and control in relation to the exchange of sex.

> **Nathan:** basically a previous friend was having issues when their parents were supposed to have hit um it was all reported to social services but the social service didn't um found it quite difficult to engage with the family and stuff and because of it um they were, trying to pimp themselves out so that they could avoid going home, um OK so stuff like that

> **Katie:** After I finished with [boyfriend] I had [drug] relapses and half a year on it [selling sex] and didn't see it as work. I felt I was in control because I was doing it for me this time not for others. It was what I had done before for money you know I thought it was normal. I haven't done it for a long time now … you're doing it for money – you're doing it to get what you need. Like even with your friends you can't keep skanking off them to help you out with anything because then no one will be your friend in the end. You need money for everything in life

Nathan and Katie talk about exchanging sex as a way of dealing with their circumstances. Nathan needed to avoid going home, so exchanged sex for somewhere to stay. Katie needed money for drugs and so exchanged sex for money to buy them. There was no grooming here. They did not talk of being 'coerced' or manipulated; neither did they identify a single or multiple abuser enticing or controlling them to engage in exchanging sex. They talked of 'pimping' themselves, 'doing it' for themselves. Katie relayed how she needed money to survive, to pay for a place to stay and to fund her drug addiction and so she 'took to the streets' to exchange sex with people as a way of getting that money. As she tells us above, she had no friends to help her out, she had no way of getting what she needed, and within such constraints she went "on it" to get money. It was something she had done before and something she knew. There were also accounts from professionals, albeit few, which aligned with this way of framing sexual exploitation. They spoke of sex as a 'transaction', as 'prostitution', and as 'renting', of young people 'doing something sexual *for something*'. As with the young people's reflections, exchanging sex was considered by some professionals as a response or a way of coping with their circumstances and unmet needs:

> **Kevin (policing):** the reality is, if your life is, not to put too fine a point on it, *shit,* and you've got nothing and no one, and someone buys you things, then you would think this isn't so bad. This is maybe why some appear to turn to prostitution, because they have something that that men, boys, teenagers will pay to get

As can be seen in Kevin's account above, there was no moral approbation of the young people's behaviour; instead they tended to speak of young people who have little support, who were in difficult circumstances for whom the exchange of sex was considered to be a 'last resort' coping mechanism:

> **Faye (third sector):** there was just very vulnerable girls, who uh, had massive drug problems, and the only way they could fund it was through prostitution, so that was what they did

Sex was also considered by some professionals as a perverse means of young people gaining or regaining a sense of power (see also O'Neill, 2001; Pearce et al, 2002; Moore, 2006; Clutton and Coles, 2007), which is something we see glimpsed in Katie's explanation earlier. Andrea's observations find some notable similarity with the views of the young people interviewed, whereby exchanging sex for money allows some sense of agency:

> **Andrea (healthcare):** I think I see a difference *between* people who are being sexually exploited and who then understand that actually, they could be a bit more businesslike about this, um, and then they will say upfront that that's their way of taking control of the situation is to say well no I'm governing this transaction, so you're not just going to give me that, you're not going to give me, fish and

> chips, I want 20 quid [pause] and this is what you'll get for
> it, so they change and they get hardened and, I think that's
> people recognising they're being sexually exploited and
> thinking well I'm going to get some money for doing this

Typically, in these accounts young people were not talked of as being
coerced or forced into exchanging sex, but this was still understood to
be a form of sexual exploitation. Young people were considered to be
'selling sex' because it was a way of coping, of asserting some control
– it was a viable option from the very few alternatives open to them.

Without resorting to some individualising reductionism, exchanging
sex in this way can be seen from these participants' point of view as an
active assertion of agency to meet needs. To deny this would be to deny
the young people's experiences as they perceive them. In so stating,
they should not be seen as somehow rational actors making rational
choices within a social vacuum free of history and context (Shaw
and Butler, 1998: 184; Pitts, 1997; Moore, 2006). Rather there were
moments when selling sex was an option to cope with some difficulty
(O'Neill, 2001). This more dynamic approach to choices and motives
acknowledges the nature of some degree of agency by young people.
In so doing, it directs attention towards the 'conditions of consent' and
why it may be that some young people decide to exchange sex (see
Pitts, 1997). Yet 'sexual exploitation' is cast by guidance as coercion
or manipulative 'grooming' as *the* explanation for why and how young
people come to exchange sex. With such an emphasis on 'grooming',
and the explicit denial of young people's ability to provide consent,
how are the specific experiences of, for example, Katie and Nathan
to be recognised given they do not 'fit' this discourse?

One conclusion could be that they were not sexually exploited as
they themselves promoted the selling of sex; the very sort of conclusion
that until relatively recently saw young people like Sarah, Nathan and
Katie positioned as offenders, out of the bounds of social care. Such a
view then would seem to be wholly implausible and we might agree
with Montgomery (1998: 149) in her assessment of similar conundrums
related to her ethnographic research in Thailand with children involved
in exchanging sex that, despite their active involvement in prostitution,
the children were 'undoubtedly exploited' and could not be construed
as engaged in anything other than harmful activities. While the young
people in this study spoke of making choices, of exchanging sex in
ways that do not fit within conceptions of grooming, the sentiment of
exploitation and abuse was present within their talk. They did not use
the term themselves yet they talked about being "groped", "degraded",

"damaged", "completely fucked up", "abused", and "used". This can be seen in Sarah's comments below:

> **Sarah:** You know secret diary of a call girl you know the TV programme have you seen it?
>
> *Sophie:* um, yeh I've not actually seen but I know of it, I've seen the adverts yeh,
>
> **Sarah:** yep, right well programmes like that shouldn't be allowed because they influence people you know make them think that's what it's like for us. Bollocks! It's *not* like that. You think you'll be earning top dollar you know. Like people watch it and think oh yeh that looks like a great job, she makes it look like a one night stand sort of thing, like it's all lovely and she's getting respect. It's nothing like that. It's TV influencing that. It's dirty horrible men disrespecting you. Down back alleys, making you do stuff … Pressure that's a big thing. People would pressure you into doing stuff that you didn't want to do. You'd get blokes, like um how it is supposed to work is that they give you the money upfront right, and then you'd get people who would say no I'll pay you after, and they'd pressure you into doing stuff. They'd know you were an addict and they'd say oh come on its late I might be the last one you're going to get tonight and then you'll have the money, or they'd say if you do this I'll give you more money at the end, and then they'd change the money you know the cost and use the drugs as bait and you'd end up doing it for them.

Sarah explains how she experienced "pressure", and was made "to do stuff" by the men who paid her for sex. The "blokes", the "dirty horrible men" with whom she exchanged sex, undoubtedly exploited her need to get money for drugs. Similarly, as discussed above, other young people described a complex and layered experience of physical, sexual and emotional abuse. Coercion, manipulation and pressure formed part of their experiences. Sarah considered herself to be choosing to 'sell sex' but yet she did not suggest or talk about this as if it were somehow a 'good' choice. Drawing attention to the coercion and pressure experienced by the young people should not detract from the point being made here, else there is a risk of reinforcing the very narrative being challenged. These were young people 'choosing' to exchange sex for something, and recourse to emphasising the abuse and violence they experienced should not be necessary for understanding their experiences as sexual exploitation. The young people talked about "the things going on", that turn of phrase representing the vulnerabilities and risks underpinning how it is that they came to exchange sex which, in turn, made more complicated or further damaged their circumstances. For example, for some, their experiences had also made them drug dependent, or had left them with little support or a place to stay. They emphasised the lack of help in their lives or how they no longer wanted the help that was offered. One way of coping and of managing such risks was to exchange sex for unmet needs. In this way, as Phoenix (2002:362) argues, the 'reasons' underpinning young people's involvement in the exchange of sex can also become 'the effects' of it'.

Sexual exploitation: 'it's people taking advantage in a sexual way'

The element of exchange is inherent to these understandings of sexual exploitation. Regardless of the exploitative context there was a perceived or actual exchange of sex for something – whether it be drink, drugs, safety, a relationship, money, avoidance of rape, a place to stay … the list goes on. But that there is an *exchange*, of some sort, taking place stands as a reminder that sexual exploitation is not a linear process. It is this which draws attention to two fundamental aspects of sexual exploitation that are essential to any full understanding of the problem: unmet needs and vulnerabilities; and young people's agency.

A consistent theme in the ways that the young people spoke of their experiences of exchanging sex was that of people taking advantage: taking advantage of "vulnerable people", of "people who"ve had hard lives", of their "needs", "emotions and feelings", and of them. As Nathan summarises below:

> **Nathan:** Um in a nutshell, it's explaining the fact that it's basically [pause] taking advantage of someone's circumstances whether it's they're emotionally damaged because of their family or whatever, or because of their sexuality and they can't express it or, whether it's uh, you know they're in dire need of money or whatever and just taking advantage in a sexual way uh, using [coughs] uh their weaknesses to get, uh, not favour 'cos that makes it sound like it's good but uh, um [pause] yeh sexual outcome

Nathan conveys the ways the young people typically conceptualised sexual exploitation. It is when someone takes advantage of a person's vulnerabilities for a "sexual outcome". A young person can be taken advantage of when they are in a position of powerlessness, for reasons that can be monetary, emotional/psychological or circumstantial. Some of the young people may not have been groomed, they may not have been coerced or had any involvement with a 'pimp' or 'boyfriend'. They may themselves have decided to exchange sex. Yet all the young people talked about their experiences as *people taking advantage* – of them or of a need they had. As considered in the previous chapters, the young people considered themselves, their inner sense of identity and needs, as invisible to family, carers and those tasked to help them who they believed saw them more as 'object', as a problem status requiring protection and oversight. They described many experiences which 'blotted out' their sense of subjective self and individuality (O'Connell Davidson, 2005: 55) whereby they found various ways in order to cope and to hide their feelings. In this way, exchanging sex, for some young people is *a* solution of sorts, or a response, to these "things going on"; that is, the sorts of problems that made them vulnerable, and subsequent difficulties arising from their own ways of coping. For some young people these sexually exploitative circumstances enabled them to feel as subject, as asserting themselves to meet needs, or having needs met. For some, in these relationships there is a perverse aspect of recognition and reciprocity in that something is wanted from them, whereas their experiences of other relationships were that neither they nor nothing they had was wanted at all. In short, the seeming contradiction of feeling in some ways visible as a person (being appreciated, looked at, 'looked after'), while also being exploited, can occur because the objectification in exchanging sex is cast as something acceptable, or a least worst option.

In this way, sexual exploitation was understood by the young people to be preventable. It is something that 'doesn't just happen'. The young people perceived that had they and their needs been acknowledged by significant others, they would not have been in these sexually exploitative situations. Instead they perceived themselves as vulnerable and without care and in order to cope they exchanged sex. This, in their view, was either inevitable, or a necessary least worst 'choice'. It became 'an uncomfortable comfortableness' for some. They perceived that no one could or would help, and spoke of being "unable to get help" or having no one to "make it all stop". They were in subtle and various ways already and made further "invisible" to those who might or should help. Thus, their needs and circumstances were exploited "in a sexual way". They may have been making decisions to exchange sex and/or they may have decided to stay in 'bad relationships' in order to cope practically and emotionally, but they were still being taken advantage of.

Yet this sense of contradiction – of using agency to consent to sex while being exploited – a capacity to make decisions even though they were sometimes 'bad' decisions, seems explicitly discounted within discourses of CSE and throughout the official guidance, in which young people are positioned as being unable to consent (see Coy, 2016). Again, I do not mean to suggest that the young people were making rational considered choices within some ideal moral and practical calculus – were such to exist. Neither is it suggested that the young people should be considered as somehow 'heroic survivors' (see for example Williams, 2010), which somehow underplays a more layered grasp of complexity in favour of a more individualised moral discourse of forbearance and courage. Nonetheless, it must be noted that young people can and do 'consent'. Their accounts considered in this chapter suggest just that and provide some insight into the paradoxical and anomalous circumstances that permeate the exchange of sex. Young people's agency, and the nature of this consent, needs to be understood, for it is only in so doing that recognition can also be given to why and how young people sometimes 'exercise it ... while on other occasions they do not' (Prout, 2000: 16). As O'Connell Davidson argues:

> many children – especially those who live in difficult circumstances – do nonetheless evaluate the choices they face on the basis of knowledge and experience ... children, as much as adults, can and do act upon the basis of their subjective evaluation of the different options available to them. (2005: 54)

Just as the young people's choices cannot be understood to have been made in a 'social vacuum' (Shaw and Butler, 1998: 184), neither can their experiences of exchanging sex be considered in isolation from other aspects of their lives (see also Warrington, 2010: 70). The problem of 'child sexual exploitation' is one that is complex and there are a number of reasons why young people become involved in sexually exploitative encounters and relationships (O'Neill, 2001; Moore, 2006; Pearce et al, 2002; Pearce, 2009). These reasons need to be grasped and acted upon by those seeking to help young people. The young people's accounts suggest that aside from grooming, understood as occurring between individuals, other psycho-socioeconomic factors such as sexuality and attitudes towards sex, material, emotional and economic needs can form part of any involvement in the exchange of sex (see also McMullen, 1987; O'Neill, 2001; Taylor-Browne, 2002; Drinkwater et al, 2004). But underlying these is the subjective self with needs, which re-frames the objectification of sexual exchange as somehow acceptable or inevitable.

The difficulties in accommodating the above sorts of experiences into an understanding of child sexual exploitation is evident in the professionals' accounts. Despite there being multiple understandings of the ways that young people may experience being sexually exploited, within and across the professionals' accounts, there was some uncertainty present in many of the accounts about precisely what this problem is. Contrary to the young people, who were clear about what they understood as being sexual exploitation, there appeared to be some confusion in the professionals' accounts, particularly related to the boundaries of this issue in regard to what counts as 'child sexual exploitation'. A point Jack summarises aptly below:

> **Jack (youth justice):** you could have the softer end of sexual exploitation with boyfriends you wouldn't be happy with, right down to the murky world of hard end sexual exploitation, so uh, it's difficult really to pinpoint it

The vagaries and multiple constructs displayed in their accounts suggests the term is understood and deployed more as some portmanteau category in which there are gradations. Child sexual exploitation was talked of as a term encompassing a range of different experiences, yet there was evidently some uncertainty about when particular experiences can be termed child sexual exploitation in some definitive sense. In short, their accounts displayed a shared sense of uncertainty about whether their worries about a young person's sexual activity and relationships could be considered as instances requiring an associated safeguarding response. Matthew considers some of the difficulties below:

> **Matthew (youth work):** again this whole, um [pause] level of what constitutes, you know, this idea that there is this idealised, you know everybody is happy lovely fluffy, which you know, in reality doesn't exist for many people so we're um, all sort of aware of what constitutes the *ideal*, and then you've sort of got this massive scale of what [long pause] what constitutes a really abusive worrying

relationship where they are being essentially pimped out by their partner to their friends, you know, being passed on, the worst worst case scenarios, and then there is that whole area in between [pause] and what would be you know in terms of, um, in our own circle of friends if we saw that, we'd be fairly concerned if we saw that even if it was fairly bottom end, but transpose that into this area and it's, um, it's not normal in terms of what *we* understand of as normal but it's normal for this area [pause] but then does that become acceptable, because it's normal or because everybody's doing it, because what happens is you start moving up the scale and, well at some point you'll move right up to the top of the scale and think oh well everybody is doing this, and just accept it

Matthew's insights represent ably some of the shared occupational difficulties faced by professionals in identifying instances of child sexual exploitation – difficulties that can arguably be traced back to the framing of the problem within policy and practice. Underpinned as it is by 'grooming', young people's involvement in the exchange of sex has become increasingly portrayed as a problem in which girls are exploited by an adult older male. A strong focus for prevention is on educating young people about healthy relationships and guidance on identification suggests looking for signs that young people are in unhealthy relationships – indeed for most professionals this was interpreted as the way of seeing the problem. Yet, as Matthew explains, unless the relationship involves groups of people – those 'worst case scenarios' – it can be difficult to know when concerns can be considered as instances of sexual exploitation. This is more complex where there is no obvious relationship at all, as can be seen in what Polly has to say below:

Polly (youth work): they could do more training on it, um yeh 'cos we've been trained on relationships and stuff um but um yeh when I worked in [part of the city] we used to come across young prostitutes and they wouldn't talk to us really and if they looked really young I mean they would always say they were 17 so they couldn't get caught but we didn't really know what to do with them

The confusion displayed by Polly is an example of the very real problem with which 'child sexual exploitation' can obscure other instances of young people exchanging sex outside of grooming from the view of professionals tasked with identifying young people in these sorts of difficulties. As O'Connell Davidson (2005: 57) considers, when sex involves young children it is clearly outside of social conventions and norms. Yet sex between young people, and young people exchanging sex 'takes us into more difficult terrain'. The 17-year-old 'prostitutes' that Polly describes, who are above the state age of consent for sex and who do not engage with services, appear to have very little to do with a 'child sexual exploitation' that is bounded by unhealthy relationships and grooming.

That these are the very sorts of young people that changes in policy were intended for lends weight to Phoenix's (2002) concerns that the language of grooming could lead to misunderstanding among professionals about who may be a victim and thus affect identification of the problem. The findings noted here suggest that there is awareness of a problem that is broader and more complex than grooming; yet there is an uncertainty about whether these are instances of 'child sexual exploitation' warranting a safeguarding response. This in turn suggests that this is a problem that is difficult to recognise and interpret, partly because there are multiple forms of sexual exploitation that are not captured by the ways in which policy and procedure encodes the phenomenon. There is an indication that certain experiences of sexual exploitation, and by extension some young people themselves – indeed the young people who took part in this study – are not easily accounted for or rendered visible within a discourse aligned to grooming relationships and the manipulation or coercion into taking part in sexual activity by an abusive *adult*. This is particularly so for those young people, such as Sarah and Katie, for whom the exchange of sex is a coping response albeit made within severely adverse circumstances. 'Grooming' as a key conceptual mode and operational model can be problematic for professionals as it does not encourage or provide a discourse to enable them to fully explain and account for how and why young people come to experience sexual exploitation. As Melrose (2012: 160) argues, 'the new semantics of 'sexual exploitation' arguably means that the concept has been stretched to the point where is has become extremely vague and therefore rather meaningless'. In this way, paradoxically, the narrowness of 'child sexual exploitation' as grooming can mean it becomes difficult to interpret.

While 'grooming' features in both sets of participants' accounts as one way of making sense of sexual exploitation, this discourse does not fully capture or recognise the ways in which the young people made sense of their experiences. As we have heard, there are many sexually exploitative experiences which fall outside of this understanding. Peer sexual exploitation, transient and/or transactional sexual exploitation, sexual exploitation within the family, sexual exploitation as sex work were all experiences of abuse through the exchange of sex or sexual activity for something. Yet, as Melrose (2012) considers, the discursive power of 'sexual exploitation', underpinned by the concept of grooming and powerless victims, means that only certain routes into the exchange of sex are now recognised (see also Phoenix, 2002; Pearce, 2006; Moore, 2006). Limited in this way, policy simplifies the phenomenon and does not much recognise needs being met through the exchange of sex (see also Melrose, 2012; Pearce, 2010). This can exclude or obscure some young people's experiences and by extension some young people themselves. The issue is simplified to one in which the experiences of individual young people become homogenised and the differences in their experiences 'are virtually obliterated by the fact of their exploitation' (Melrose, 2012: 4). They *cannot* in some informed or authentic sense consent, ergo they must have been forced into it. As such, and building on the discussion in previous chapters also, the young people as real subjective actors become invisible within policy and guidance in three ways. First, the complexities of their emotional and social worlds are not well illuminated by the grooming discourse if at all. Second, their subjective capacity for agency and choice is considered inauthentic and falsely informed. Third, their different individual circumstances are obscured or occluded from policy and popular understanding and discourse by the broad cloak of 'exploitation'. The problem of sexual exploitation is thus simplified and thereby permits the promise of 'easy solutions' (Day, 2009: 1). Solutions which, as I now turn to consider, may not help young people, and worse, may compound their difficulty. It is this narrow construction of the problem that determines the identification, referral and responses that seek to solve or moderate the issue at hand, and it is to these that this exploration now turns.

Notes

[1] In the mid to late 2000s a number of reports, research articles and book were titled in such a way that made reference to the hidden nature of this issue, the lack of public awareness and professional understanding, and ignorance (see for example Coles, 2005; Pearce, 2009).

[2] See Chapter One for a brief discussion on the conceptual differences between international definitions of the commercial sexual exploitation of children and child sexual exploitation.

3   As I considered in Chapter One, in Wales the link between grooming and the term sexual exploitation is more explicit, with the definition making a direct reference to grooming.

FIVE

Responses, recognition and reciprocity

The introduction of 'child sexual exploitation' to social care policy and practice has ensured that the issue is now a safeguarding priority and a child protection concern. While preventative measures focus on reducing risks and educating children and young people about 'healthy relationships' and matters of consent, responses to young people caught up in sexual exploitation can include intensive support work or, at the sharp end, removing them to foster care or secure residential units for their protection. This chapter considers what the participants had to say about how best to respond to sexual exploitation and to children and young people involved in it. It may not be too obvious to state that in so doing, they are also telling us about the very nature of the problem itself. As Williams (2010) notes, solutions are intricately connected to the problem. What the problem of sexual exploitation is understood to be determines 'who' and 'what' is of concern and the necessary responses employed. Here a number of the themes considered in previous chapters arise again, such as care, unmet needs and the conceptual parameters of the problem. The chapter considers the importance of recognition, reciprocity and interdependency within care relationships, and also signals to the need to acknowledge the wider context surrounding sexual exploitation. The discussion begins by hearing from the young people, and their thoughts on the focus of interventions.

"Just don't come in with the solutions until you've analysed the problem!"

As is emphatically declared by Leah in the quote above, if we are to begin to consider the possible 'solutions' to CSE, we must first make sure that we have a clear idea of what the problem is. Leah's statement was made in reference to support for her individual circumstances, yet it is also an apt summary of the ways the young people talked about responses to CSE in general. Their accounts conveyed a sense of frustration that people hadn't quite grasped the complexities of the issue:

Nathan: people don't, sometimes I think they just see the outside of it and they don't give enough time to focus on what's happening on the inside, you know discovering what the vulnerabilities are, to, um, also to make sure that they don't fall into it [pause] as I said, I don't think it [sexual exploitation] starts with a young person needing to do it or being tricked or forced into sex, I think it's at the point where, you're becoming vulnerable to getting to that stage.

As Nathan's explanation conveys, for adults to provide support, they must first understand that sexual exploitation is not something that can be de-contextualised from other aspects of their lives. It is constitutive of those 'things going on', discussed in Chapters Two and Three. The young people's underlying vulnerabilities, by which they meant their feelings of instability and uncertainty, difference and exclusion, confused boundaries about sex and ownership over their bodies, sense of agency, and their invisibility to family, carers and those tasked to help them, are not just indicators of the problem – they *are* the problem. From young people's perspectives, without these underlying unmet needs and issues there would be nothing to take advantage of, no vulnerability or need to exploit for sex. The young people did not seek to diminish the significance of their experiences of being sexually exploited, yet their accounts spoke much more to the need for carers, parents, those tasked to help them, to focus their attention on these difficulties as being part of the problem. In talking about their experiences, the young people suggested that people do not give enough attention to the reasons why 'it' may be happening or recognise that these reasons form part of the 'it' itself. The frustrations expressed by the young people about this, suggested an awareness that they and those tasked to help them had a different understanding of their experiences. They spoke of how people "make sexual exploitation too simple" and "not broad enough"; of how "people think you're not being taken advantage of if you're not being pimped out"; of how "people need to see the more subtle side" such as the controlling and manipulative side of abusive relationships. There is a further sense of this in what Leah and Sarah have to say, below:

Leah: more emotionally type reasons don't seem to come into it

Sarah: people think you're not at risk until you've started doing it

Hannah: my foster carer actually *did* a sexual exploitation uh they actually *did* a course on it, while I was with the partner I was with, I don't think she knew what I was up to or what to be looking for really

As Hannah tells us, without this more complex understanding of the problem, people will not be able to 'see' when it is happening. If the underlying needs and vulnerabilities are considered to be the real risk and the problem that needs to be dealt with, then those things the young people did to cope – their use of alcohol and drugs, their hiding away and 'hanging out', their 'sleeping around' – could be seen as signs of this anterior problem. They talked of how this is not often picked up by those charged with helping them, who instead focus on those behaviours rather than on taking the time to understand what the real problems are that they are dealing with. People don't see 'it' because people don't 'see' young people. Kerry aptly summarises this:

Kerry: I think it might be because they are sometimes *overseen* [pause] like um the issues that young people face [pause] aren't [pause] aren't always dealt with. Like people can be dealing with things internally, and no one not many people have *the time*, or put the time in to find out *what's really going on* [pause] they just see the *surface exterior* and they never try and pursue further to see what the actual person is dealing with

To point to Kerry's last sentence above, she speaks of how there is an "actual person" – a young person who has depths that are not perceived – who is dealing with things, who is unacknowledged by the carers and professionals around them. A point the young people were concerned to make is that relevant adults do not seem to give the time to find out and address what a young person is feeling or dealing with; instead it is often their behaviour which comes to notice, leaving them feeling further ignored, leaving them to continue to cope and deal with these 'things' in the ways they have been.

This has consequences in that key adults do not see the problem for what it is, because they do not see the underlying matters that young people are dealing with. According to the young people, this aspect of being overlooked or missed compounds the problem in that they come to believe they are left to cope on their own. Furthermore, in believing they are ignored, some young people feel unable to share their experiences. Thus, paradoxically, they may hide themselves emotionally and physically because they come to think of themselves and their problems as invisible anyway. Any response requires insight into a young person's sense of self and their common sense understandings of their social realities in order to begin to respond in the ways that person needs (see O'Connell Davidson, 2005). Moreover, without this, and without dealing with these underlying issues, there is a risk of compounding the problem. As Nathan clearly and succinctly tells us:

> **Nathan:** I don't know I think, sometimes I think it can be too, um [pause] slightly too, um, sometimes too strictly and sometimes too harshly, um I think that sometimes people try to *pull* others out of situations that are bad for them which is *good* in a sense, but I think that sometimes, *sometimes not always*, but I think that when people try to *pull* them out *really quickly* that sometimes, if it's an emotional issue, it can sometimes *cause* them damage as well because they haven't, even if it's an unhealthy outlet they haven't dealt with that and so it can just be redirected somewhere else and cause more issues for them somewhere else ... try and work on the issues that make them vulnerable to it, and then as they become as their life becomes a bit more stable, um hopefully they should be able to withdraw from, what is making turn towards that ... sometimes I think they try to deal with sexual exploitation on its own, and I think that, it can sometimes sort itself temporarily but the underlying issue needs to be, *dealt* with as well otherwise they might just come back to it, and sometimes I think that, unless um, yeh the underlying issues are dealt with, and you may not be able to get to them when you start off but they can just quite easily fall into the risk of doing it again

As Nathan explains, 'sexual exploitation' may not be the greatest risk for a young person and it cannot be separated out from the other difficulties a young person is facing. The underlying issues have to be dealt with. Katie relayed how she was placed in a secure unit as the response to her sexual exploitation when she was living with her boyfriend, and she talked about her experiences of being the unit in ways that sat in parallel with the ways she spoke about her experiences of being sexually exploited. She described feeling controlled, her movements monitored, an environment of hostility characterised by outbursts of violence. This was her experience of secure care. Yet in this care, for her protection, there were no drugs, there was no one who she perceived as looking after her in some way, and there was nothing needed from her. Katie described needing help with her drug addiction, before she could even begin to feel different about her sexual exploitation in the immediate term. While for the longer term, she described needing help and support to deal with deep-rooted feelings of insecurity, alongside more practical help and advice in how to live differently so that 'the streets' were not her go-to solution.

The importance of support: "It was having someone who was there for me…"

All the young people talked of their needing and wanting support. It is perhaps telling that they did not talk much about the content of this help. They did not have much to say about what people should *do* in any practical sense, or much about *who* should support them. Instead they spoke of needing '*someone* there', as Sarah intimates about a particular person:

> **Sarah:** I think it's 'cos she's someone who's there and she makes sure I'm alright you know, she lets me know I'm okay

When Katie tells us of her relationship with her social worker, she reiterates a similar message:

> **Katie:** When [name] became my social worker. She did it all, she did everything for me, she was there for me, she set everything up, she took me under her wing really.

As considered in previous chapters, the young people typically invoked a lack of care which they experienced as instability and insecurity, uncertainty and difference. They described feelings of relative powerlessness over their circumstances and a profound sense of insecurity in not having some durable, safe, caring habitus of people and place (see Pitts, 1997). In this sense the problem can be captured in terms of unpredictability and chaos. When everything feels insecure, and unstable, it is 'support', having someone *there*, that they craved; someone seemingly solid and immovable in a world of turmoil. Danny provides a sense of this:

> **Danny:** I don't know, just the support I think, I'm glad for the support you know, someone helping me, because

if I didn't have this, I'd probably be, I don't know, I don't know where I'd be. I'm just glad for the support really.

The word 'support' means to bear, to hold, to shoulder, to stay, to keep from falling. Its meaning is laboured here to bring into focus the poignancy of the young people's reflections on their experiences of support from family and those tasked to help them. We have heard throughout the young people speak of "being thrown in the deep end", of "falling into it" because there was no one else there, of needing "someone to make it stop". They spoke of feeling uncared for, ignored, unnoticed, taken advantage of and used. What they wanted was to have someone there to support them. It was the young people's relationships with their workers – in most cases with one specific worker – which determined whether their sense of security was enhanced or not, and whether change was experienced in a more positive way. The young people all spoke of wanting help and support. Through a direct and inferred vocabulary all the young people talked of wanting to 'move on', 'move on with things', of 'moving away', of 'moving forwards' as an accomplishment of distance – emotional, physical and temporal – from the problem. Yet change may not always be experienced positively – even if desired – if change and feelings of instability sit at the root of the problem. The young people emphasised that it was having someone there which was the source of a necessary security through which change had been possible. It is as if, as Adey (2006: 86) explains, 'social life and the complexities of life seem to require immobile moorings that are solid, static and immobile' adding that 'there can be no movement without context, without something to push off from'. Thus anchored to someone, the young people could feel more certain in themselves and able to move on in a positive way. The meanings the young people attributed to support and to their movement on and away from the problem can be found in the 'embeddedness' of the relationship – its certainty, and capacity for promoting change (Adey, 2006: 83). In this way, movement experienced as 'moving on', something positive, as opposed to chaos and uncertainty, was linked to whether the young person felt supported and in control of such change. As discussed next, it is this that marks out the importance of interdependence within the supportive relationship.

"She doesn't just do it for the job": interdependence and reciprocity

A significant related theme was that of the importance of the participants' relationships with authority figures and those tasked to care for them. All their accounts tell of the importance of feeling that there is some personal investment in that caring relationship beyond it just being someone's job. Many of the young people expressed frustration towards people just 'doing their job', a point which can be noted in Claire's account:

> **Claire:** social workers they go round and they're doing their *job*. When they say I know how you feel, they seriously don't, because when you've had this done to you, you just feel like, what's worth living for like

People who just 'do their job' were spoken of as being "unreliable", "patronising" and "make you jump through hoops". They were cast as people who "don't really want to know", "don't know what to do with you", "don't really care" and "don't want to bother". As Claire goes on to say:

> **Claire:** just don't muck them about, because if you muck the child about they'll just do something drastic and they won't know what to do, because they can't turn to you if you're mucking them about, and saying I know how you feel, and they don't, but if someone turned to me and said I need your help I'm being sexually exploited, can you please help me, then *one* I'd turn up if they asked me to do that, *two* I know how they're feeling because I've been there, and *three* I know I'd help them

Claire's troubling account conveys how the phrase 'just doing the job' stands for so much. It represents indifference and a lack of empathy. It is to feel dependent on people who do not care about them. It is to be reminded that the only people who care do so because they are paid to, not because they want to. This conveys a feeling of being the object of concern and not recognised as an authentic other, of being seen but not seen; of people seeing but not seeing (Sennett, 2003: 171). That is, the young people spoke of feeling only of interest because of their objectified need; of people knowing all manner of details about their lives but not knowing them as a person. People who just do their job made the young people feel powerless and unwanted. Similarly, people who *really care* are people who do more than their job, as Katie tells us:

> **Katie:** like I love my social worker she really helped me, been there for me – she's like my best friend ... she makes

sure I'm alright. She doesn't just do it for the job, she does things for me when she's not working

Similarly to Katie, the young people used the language of family and friendship to make sense of the relationships they had with people which they felt were positive. They spoke of people who are *like* family, *like* a best friend, someone they could get on *with*, and someone they had fun *with*. Yet poignantly the young people were not describing people who were like their actual family and friends but rather their ideal of family and friends. For example, Sarah described how her support worker was "like a mum, not like my mum". Furthermore, people who do more than their job were spoken of as being "trustworthy", "safe", "easy to talk to" and "friendly". In so doing, they were drawing on ideas of unconditional relationships in which there was meaning and commitment from both parties. This finds a strong parallel with literature arguing that relationships are core to child-centred practice and to 'good' social work (see Holland, 2010; Winter, 2010). The young people's accounts indicate the importance of mutuality and interdependency in their relationships with their carers and those tasked to help them. This can be seen within the examples given by Nathan and Leah below, in which they spoke of instances that stood out for them as being particularly special or helpful:

> **Nathan:** one of my support workers who would always like take me for coffee and I'd have hot chocolate and they'd have coffee and it was kind of like, kind of like a safe environment for me, somewhere where I felt less, stressed and they kind of, we would work on issues but it was more like, we'd *talk* about an issue, and then maybe when we had done that we would move on to something else not work, and just things like that really, I liked that way that, you know it wasn't too bogged down and horribly serious.

As Nathan observes, 'getting the work done' is dependent on a relationship that exists as more than the 'job' itself, indeed it is the relationship which forms the work. Leah conveys something similar:

> **Leah:** When we went to the um cinema I really liked that

> *Sophie:* What was it you liked about it?

Leah: 'Cos it all went dark and just as it was going to start she goes BOO [laughs] I jumped, I jumped a mile, it was so funny, and she was making me laugh and I was making her laugh and um. She's weird. She's quite good at sort of messing around and being fun. She like, makes, doing work with her she makes it different, she don't make you do it, but like on the other hand other people do, so it's different. She like, it feels like we are just hanging out.

What can be seen in both Nathan and Leah's accounts is an appreciation of those instances in which the relational aspect of care takes precedence over those formal aspects of work which simply need to occur procedurally. The young people emphasised the importance of being recognised and being acknowledged as more than their need. Not only that, but within these examples and in others like the above, the young people emphasised the importance of interdependency, giving emphasis to seemingly small instances of reciprocity, an example of which is shared by Katie:

Katie: We, I was 7 we went down to the pier you know down in [name] and I ran ahead to the swings and this was with [name of worker] and you know that the pier has those holes in it like where the slats are? Well I looked back and she had stopped still halfway down and she was so scared she couldn't go any further and couldn't go back, she was so scared she couldn't move. I was 7 years old and I had to go back and hold her hand and help her back off the pier [laughs]

Sophie: [laughs] ah, that's a nice story. What was it about that time that was so special for you?

Katie: *she* trusted *me*. I was holding *her* hand.

For the young people to feel safe and cared for there must be a degree of mutuality and reciprocity as indicated above. It is in reciprocal relationships which implicitly acknowledge the interdependency of care relationships that the young people felt present as active subjects, and not just objects of concern. As such, reciprocal care and interest was creating a new subjectivity in that their feelings of loneliness, isolation, their feeling unwanted and of notice to no one were counteracted in some way by the relationship itself.

115

"It's the talking that's important, that's what helps really, just talking"

All the young people emphasised the importance of talk. In fact, aside from identifying support and relationships, 'talking to someone' was the only other source of significant impact they identified. The young people described how it is through talk that they and their experiences can be discovered behind the surface exterior and made visible. They explained that it is through talk that people can make sense of the things that they *do*; because it is through talking that they can share how they felt. This insight, while seemingly obvious, belies the difficulty in disclosing their histories and conveys that this is likely to occur only when there is trust and mutuality. By sharing how they felt, people would be able to *see* what the problems for them are. They spoke of the need to bring up to the surface the ways that they felt, and the things that were going on in their lives. Nathan makes the point succinctly:

> **Nathan:** this might sound really simple, but the idea that someone, when, the issues arise is there, and this is a good thing about the [name] service, is when the thing is out that the worker really takes the time to try and understand the details of what it is that you are going through

Despite participants speaking of how it is talking that helps, most of what they had to say in interview was about the ways that talking can be *unhelpful*, as Nathan also goes on to say:

> **Nathan:** yeh, where I was being asked question and it wasn't like, it wasn't done in a very sensitive manner, it was very um thing you know it was very, they were so direct that it wasn't, you couldn't, you wouldn't feel comfortable answering, and I think that [pause] yeh, too direct questions can be an issue, I think that things need to be brought up gently, yeh ... they never [pause] treat every person with the kind of attitude of learning their trust first and get them to open up about the issues that *really* face them, they're faced with, 'cos, I think sometimes professionals expect young people to just sometimes just lay it on a plate for them yeh, and then tell them that there's a billion and one things wrong [pause] but it's not like that, it's normally it's difficult for them to tell people, um yeh that's about it [pause] yeh

The participants explained how being "made to talk", being "made to go over and over things", being made to "bring up the bad stuff" made them feel worse. When they had to provide a certain type of account, when their story wasn't theirs to tell in the way they wanted, or when they were ready, it made them feel as passive objects – unheard and unacknowledged.

The institutional and forensic practices of child protection frequently create an adversarial and intrusive context (see Wastell et al, 2010). Professionals are required to perform an excavation of the 'facts', of what went on, but in so doing risk leaving a young person feeling as an object of concern, a victim of abuse, seen only for their need. Accordingly, the participants perceived this official concern more as professional indifference to them as unique individuals, and this reinforced a sense of powerlessness, of being 'unseen' and unacknowledged as a person. Danny sought to express this experience as follows:

> **Danny:** um *labels*, I think um, some people um people do say sometimes oh you're like *that* because of *this*. They don't really know that do they you know, for a fact, like they've got to listen more like. I've spoke to people and they've just sat there and they haven't listened to me and then I'm going no because I'm not like that because of that and I get frustrated like … even if they might be right, you still want to tell it, to be able to talk about it 'cos they might not be [right].

Danny's account was typical of responses across the sample. They spoke of frustrations when people did not listen to them. They spoke of feeling unheard and of how people were not interested in what *they* had to say about their experiences. As Claire explains, this sense of indifference can feel like speaking to a "brick wall":

> **Claire:** I've noticed that with a few social workers I just feel like I'm talking to a brick wall
>
> *Sophie:* …in what sort of way?
>
> **Claire:** they listen but *it's like a false listening*, they just write it on a piece of paper and, you know we'll deal with it sort of thing but you're not getting any sense of understanding of it.

Claire uses a common idiom (a brick wall) but it is one that is powerful in symbolising the shared perception of unresponsiveness, of professionals not listening, not caring. There is self-evidently no authentic relationship with a person who is like a brick wall. Claire expressed anger about her experiences of care and support. She could not say anything positive about the support she had received, and throughout her interview spoke often of feeling misunderstood:

> **Claire:** the kid may actually flip out, and just say *sorry you don't know how I feel* and blah blah blah blah blah, and then gets even more angry and that will be the cycle, and then the kid will think, what the hell am I doing here, I'm trying to tell them how I feel, *and they don't believe me* [her emphasis] so then the self-esteem goes down and down and down, and they've got no one to talk to then

Claire conveyed strong feelings of frustration and anger towards those adults presuming to know how she felt by simply garnering this information from elsewhere or from having sought the external 'facts' surrounding the problem from Claire. This, in her view, denied her the opportunity to explain and make sense of what happened in a meaningful way for herself. This attempt by professionals to construct and define the problem in their terms made her feel misunderstood and silenced her. Claire concluded that adults don't listen, don't understand and don't believe what young people say. This is particularly troubling given that Claire explained how she went online "just for someone to talk to", and in doing so was groomed by someone who sought to exploit her by raising her self-esteem. It might seem paradoxical to suggest that the young people hide their feelings, or reject help because they feel unseen and overlooked. Yet they spoke of doing just this. They wanted help but they were loath to share personal details and reluctant to disclose how they felt inside to professionals and carers they did not really know or trust.

> **Katie:** people need to spend time talking to them to find out what's really going on, what they really need you know. I said I didn't want help but I needed it.

> **Danny:** um, talking about it, that helps, just like being able to talk to them about it. And even if they don't talk about it, it will come out eventually like I've been like that, so

just being quiet and um, 'cos you trust you get trust in that
person then, *after you've seen them for a while* they'll talk more

What Danny and Katie had to say reinforced what other participants
had to say about the importance of supportive, interdependent
relationships. As McMullen (1987) has argued, trust can be a
therapeutic intervention in itself. When people 'spend time', when
they show they are there, when they show they are investing something
in the relationship, the young people felt able to ask for or accept help.
For talking to be helpful, it must be a process of openness and mutuality
between two people, and not a 'one-sided' search for the secrets of
some abusive encounter. It is not enough for young people to have
time to disclose to someone ready and willing to listen to them, it is
about talk as constituting a more interdependent encounter in which
young people can choose if, when and how they share the issues that
concern them. This implies a more open-ended and equal relationship
based on mutual regard:

> **Danny:** it goes both ways [pause] like I hate the idea of
> people just sitting there staring at me where they're waiting
> for me to say something, like you know, what am I supposed
> to say and then you get nervous and think oh I'm not going
> to be able to say anything

> **Kerry:** I hate my counselling, I don't think that helped at
> all. Because I've dealt with most of it myself. I think going
> over and over it again it's just making it worse. They just
> sitting there and it's um, I just want to be able to draw a
> line under it and move on, and it's like, you can't

While the young people spoke of the importance of people listening,
and "taking the time" to understand and "find out what was going on"
this was not always deemed helpful unless there was a relationship in
which the young person could choose what to share and how to do this:

> **Kerry:** you've got to move on really so just keep on talking
> to people, and the more you talk to people the more you
> come to your senses about what went on really … Well
> I haven't been in the situation since I came along with
> [worker's name]. She helped me to get myself out of my
> own situation. And I talk to her a lot about the stuff that
> have happened. It's been helpful just to talk to someone

that I didn't know from before, just to be able to talk to
them about it all without them knowing about me first…

As can be glimpsed above, in order to feel recognised as a person,
those tasked to help them must also be part of the process of talking,
and present within the relationship, able to work at the pace of the
young person, and not make assumptions about the needs to be met,
but working through the concerns and priorities of the young person.
Through the process of talking with another about their experiences
the young people were able to move on, because 'just talking' in a
trusting relationship is the way they are able to contemplate some
kind of change. As Pithouse et al (2011) argue, it is in a relational and
iterative exchange of knowledge that social workers and young people
can create trusting exchanges that make up the work *itself*. The young
people spoke of "needing to see things differently", and "needing to
stop and see what you hadn't seen before". The importance of time
and trust, of professionals allowing young people space to explore
events and to move at their own pace, was noted by participants and
articulated by Nathan thus:

> **Nathan:** I think I found that quite useful because I didn't
> feel like, I was just going, oh this is my problem, and them
> just I don't know jumping into it but they were just kind of
> like, waited to understand, and then they started to, help me
> re-programme things, and I think that was good [pause] so
> just showing them, what's happening and trying to explain
> it as well, keep them in the know, keep them from being
> too blurred by their own issues and things, um, yeh

As Alexander and Charles (2009: 10) argue, 'it is within relationships that
both parties influence the construction of the meaning of any event'.
The young people's perceptions of themselves and their uncertainties
about sexual boundaries and relationships were disrupted in some way
by these relationships in which they felt acknowledged, listened to and
understood. By 'seeing' other people's perspectives of themselves and
their situations, 'the ways things are' could be understood as being not
necessarily the way things had to be (see Fox, 2012).

The importance the young people attributed to 'talking' occurs
precisely because it is doing something more than just talking. It
allows for the co-construction of meaning in which the young people
were enabled to make sense of their experiences. Talking is important
because it makes sexual exploitation and the young people visible. This

happens when talking allows a young person control over content and meaning, which is listened to without the false empathy that can make them feel objectified as some collection of needs. In considering a large body of research arguing that young people do not feel listened to, are not taken seriously and are not involved in decisions about their care, Winter (2010: 194) calls for spaces to 'be created within the context of meaningful relationships with social workers for young people to express their knowledge and make sense of their circumstances. This in turn would enable a deeper understanding of what is significant' to them. It is within the context of such relationships that the young people explained they were able to share their experiences and make themselves visible.

Disclosure or exposure?

Another significant theme was the importance of people's reactions to disclosure. What people do when they initially 'find out' really seemed to matter to the young people:

> **Leah:** It's just like being able to talk about stuff, things, where they're not going to run off and tell other people and start gossiping and stuff like that, I mean she [support worker] doesn't give a reaction and if she does it's always a positive one she's not like [pause] *oh my god* and make you feel like, oh I must be bad if her reaction's that

Leah's account is typical in that interviewees often spoke of the importance of professionals and carers not being "shocked", not "over-reacting", and of the need for such adults to stay calm about what they heard. They were concerned about the judgements people may make about them, and they particularly invoked the importance of confidentiality. They spoke of experiences of having been rejected by significant others in their lives because of public knowledge about their involvement in sexual exploitation. Hence they were now guarded about who they would trust with disclosures about their lives:

> **Claire:** School, that's important. If you talk to your teachers about information about this or this sort of thing, um, then you tell them there's something going on in your life, that's a bad situation because then they'll involve the police and parents and you don't want to be in that situation

Sophie: OK OK, so school is bad because teachers aren't necessarily people you can trust?

Claire: yeh [pause] and it might not stay confidential in the school you see, and plus when you're in the school you've got your friends as well, who will find out and they disown you basically [pause] if you haven't got someone to talk to, organise an appointment with the doctors and speak to them because they have to listen and it's confidential.

Without a relationship of trust with those they spoke to, the young people could not be certain of how the disclosed information about themselves would be perceived, and indeed how *they* would be perceived. Yet they spoke of the need to talk to someone to get help. Claire identifies the doctor–patient relationship as a safe area for sharing information in those instances when there is no one else to talk to. This issue of finding a trusting medium in which to feel acknowledged, heard and understood arose frequently in interviews. The initial 'disclosure' of sexual exploitation can be considered as the sharp end of this, and one in which it was important for them not to become the object of some care discourse in which *they* were not seen or where they had no control over what was understood and defined. It was critical for them to have some control over what was being revealed and when. As Sennett (2003: 117) considers, shame occurs when we are denied or lose the ability to control the conditions in which we are seen or not seen; when someone is 'rendered visible and yet is not yet ready to be visible'. There is a tension the young people have to manage between wanting relevant adults to know about their situations because they need help and the potential to feel ashamed by people's reactions, and of being 'known' by others who become party to that information and not by the young people's choosing. The importance of this point, and how this exposure of personal information can be experienced, can be seen in what Sarah and Hannah have to say below, in which they convey similar concerns about 'being known' by abusers and others related to that abuse, with the same sorts of anxieties and concern that they and others expressed about 'being known' by professionals becoming party to their intimate details:

Sarah: I've known what they're like. Even now I'll see them and they'll be with all their family but it's the way they'll look at you. Even now they'll be looking at me 'cos they know

> **Hannah:** like they could have photos of him like um doing stuff then they'll probably um, what's the word um, use it against him and send them to his family and friends, all the photos um, so he has to be careful about that

This was similar to Claire, who explained how she was afraid photographs of her, taken by the person who exploited her, would be shown to others: these photographs of her were now possibly "out there" and she had no control over whether and what people might see them.

Individuals have a need to be both visible and invisible. There is a need to feel 'seen' and known in order to feel connected to people, and yet a person also needs to feel they are not too transparent; that they can 'keep themselves to themselves'. When someone cannot control where they are positioned within this binary, it can leave them feeling 'exposed' or 'denied'. Young people in particular can find themselves positioned at the extremes of this binary; lacking authority or the position to control who knows what about them. This is particularly so for young people involved with statutory social services, in which procedures demand that information is gathered and shared by professionals working with young people to ensure they receive the protection, care and support they are entitled to. Yet it is a fear of 'being known' that can mean young people do not ask for the help they need. In essence, when young people do not have established trusting relationships, to ask for help is to risk exposure. It is for this reason that some young people suggested it could be more helpful to speak to adults who did not know them at all, did not know their names, and did not know who they were:

> **Hannah:** sometimes some people find it easier just talking to blank strangers, um [pause] with no names you don't need to tell them your name or their name or whatever, um [pause] and they can't pass anything on because they don't know your name or where they got it from

This is an aspect remarked upon by a number of young people who spoke of the importance of not having "a reputation", of needing to be unknown to move on, to feel unashamed, or to be "someone different". For example, Katie described how in 'moving on' it was important to feel visible *and* invisible, and to have some control, or perceived control, over this:

Sophie: what made you feel differently about the work?

Katie: I don't know

Sophie: do you or did you feel differently about yourself?

Katie: yeh. I moved up to [place name] you know where I met my boyfriend, and he doesn't need to know about my past. Up there I don't have a reputation. I can be who I want, I can be anything that I want. I can be a hairdresser you know, that's what I want to be.

Such reflections from the participants reveal something of the troubling complexity behind the claims within policy that 'disclosure of this form of abuse is exceptionally rare' (WAG, 2011: 27). Young people, like anyone, need 'to control the conditions under which they see and are seen' (Sennett, 2003: 118). For these young people in positions of vulnerability, talking about their experiences and abuse was sometimes experienced as both exposure and denial; of feeling as object, known only for one's need; of feeling ignored as a person by those same people who know personal intimate details about oneself. Alternatively, it was experienced as safe disclosure and preservation of self; of feeling as subject, one who is acknowledged, respected and understood. In a similar way, the young people felt objectified by perceived feelings of indifference from those tasked to care and support them. Yet the opposite, to feel pitied – that enemy of respect – in which a young person can be objectified through assumptions about their dependence and weakness, was something spoken of as equally harmful. Young people who are able to *manage* the conditions in which they relay and discuss their personal details and experiences can perceive this as a therapeutic form of disclosure whereby they feel acknowledged and visible in a way that is positive, and which is an essential prerequisite in tackling the problem itself. It is the person's control over what they reveal, how it is revealed and with whom these details are shared that makes the difference for a young person.

"It's not about throwing money at it"

Having heard from the young people, we have reached a fitting point at which to introduce the adult participants' reflections on what should be done to respond to the problem. The responses to the problem of child sexual exploitation offered by the professionals mirror much of what the young people had to say about solutions. As we will hear, while they were invited to speak about how they or others should respond to any aspect of the problem, much of what they disclosed focused on ways to respond to the needs of young people. The solutions by definition tend to collect around the need for vulnerable young people to have someone who will *care* – provide protection *and* support – as a way of safeguarding them from those who might exploit them. In this way, the narratives of the professionals centred on individual young people, and their particular need for support and protection. They did not, for example, say much about targeting the adult men, predators and boys, who they typically invoked as exploiting young people. Neither did they focus their occupational gaze on wider, more structural concerns, such as poverty, education, employment and housing. However, as will be apparent in much of the data, in many ways they *did* speak of wider problems, in that their depictions of the very structures of official care and interventions revealed their implication in the problem itself.

Structure and security

A significant theme arising from the data was the need for young people to have structure and security in their lives. Many participants emphasised the importance of the home environment, as Max below considers:

> **Max (children's residential care):** Ideally you want to take all these children and place them in a nice secure family

The professionals talked of the need for young people to be in 'normal loving homes' – homes with boundaries, rules and 'well-adapted adults' who are able to respond to young people in loving, caring ways. Much of what they spoke of was related to concerns about the adequacy of statutory care settings, particularly residential care, to provide the environment and family setting to meet the needs of young people (see also Kerrigan-Lebloch and King, 2006), mainly because those working in residential care are unable to act in the ways they would as parents. For example, Louisa (social worker) explained how placing a young person in foster care is better than placing them in residential care because it is more like home. She went on to consider how foster care is "a protective factor" for young people, because foster carers are more able "to control where young people went and what they did". They can set boundaries and know where a young person is. Cathy, below, makes a similar assessment for young people who are not in statutory care:

> **Cathy (fostering):** we need to equip parents with the knowledge and confidence to take a more proactive role in being parents and in setting boundaries

A necessary way of responding to the problem is to ensure that young people are given clear boundaries to help them to protect themselves; while those boundaries, when monitored by family, caregivers and professionals, also protect young people from those who might harm them (Pearce, 2009). In a similar way, the professionals also spoke of the need to provide and monitor boundaries in young people's day-to-day lives. They spoke of the need to give young people "positive and constructive things to do to give them some structure", to "replace the pattern of behaviour that leads to sexual exploitation", and to "gradually *push* it out" (the risky behaviour). This notion of structure and diversion can be seen in Linda's comments:

> **Linda (community work):** I was trying to get one of them involved in education, because she wasn't going to school, and there was a placement in [place name] so she was going along to that, which gave her a structure which was quite *good* which she didn't have, I think you know before she had a lot of free time and so, she was able to um or um I suppose she didn't have much to *do* and so she might as well go off and, enjoy herself with these guys

As with Linda, most participants referred to protecting young people by deploying techniques of diversion. Structuring a young person's day should ensure they are kept safe and distanced from sexually exploitative situations, or from engaging in risky behaviours, as Carla explains:

> **Carla (children's residential care):** I thought uh the best thing to do is to prevent her from *really from going out,* not locking her in but, *engaging* her in activities like I was happy for her to go to the cinema, you know just take her *away* from *that*

In so doing, the professionals spoke of how by controlling and directing the things that young people did, they hoped that they would "grow out of it", "find another way" or "think again", and exploitative relationships and patterns of behaviour would be relinquished or dissipate. Underpinning the theme considered here is that of *young people's* need of protection – protection that can be given through structure and security. As Marie outlines:

> **Marie (third sector):** we need to protect them in order to give these young people the opportunity to stabilise

The shared occupational assumption across interviews was that young people need someone watching over them who will enforce rules and boundaries – someone who will protect them from others, while also providing 'spaces', physical and temporal, to enable young people to think again about the relationships and circumstances in which they are involved. This view shares many similarities with the young people's reflections about how they were taken advantage of because of particular vulnerabilities, not least the absence or ineffectiveness of protective adults. It may be recalled that Chapter Two revealed how young people spoke of the lack of security and boundaries within their family and home settings as contributing to vulnerabilities. They also spoke of their exclusion from key institutions (such as home and school) as generating a sense of difference – that they were not quite 'normal', not like other children and young people. Yet, while the young people considered their lack of boundaries and rules to form part of the problem, they did not speak of their need for this when they talked about solutions. As we have just heard, while the need for stability featured in the young people's accounts, they considered that this stability came from people, relationships, having someone there, and if those tasked to help and care for them only focus on monitoring their behaviour and on formal procedures for protecting them, they are likely to feel further vulnerable.

Support

Many of the professionals talked of the need for young people to have support in the same way that the young people considered the meaning of the term. In strikingly similar ways, they too spoke of the need for young people to have and know that there is *someone there* for them. As Cathy explains further:

> **Cathy (fostering):** they need to be at the point where they are *willing* to work with somebody and *willing* to make changes if you're asking them to change a pattern of

behaviour then you need to have something good to put it in place, you can't just say you know that's not good don't do that [laughs] ... um, we need to, people who actually *come* alongside young people and are able to befriend them but it involves spending *a lot* of time with the young person to show them another way, um, I'm not thinking getting the right words but, but they're offering [pause] support in a way that always goes the extra mile

As Cathy says, to *support* a young person is to come alongside them. 'Going the extra mile' is the way of showing a young person that the person helping them is someone who does more than the job, is someone who is there for them. Many participants spoke of how young people involved in sexually exploitative situations are often outside of mainstream support systems, and are unlikely to have the networks available to other young people to call on when they are in difficulty. They also talked about how these young people are often the very sorts of young people who are least emotionally equipped to deal with difficulty in constructive ways (see also McMullen, 1987; O'Neill 2001). Participants typically invoked common sense notions of care, such as, the need for young people to have 'someone to hold their hand', someone who would get them out of bed in the morning, a familiar someone to meet them and make sure they get to the places they need to be, such as appointments, work placements, health visits. Through these acts of practical support, these 'everyday acts of care' (see Holland, 2010: 173), over time, a relationship could be established with a young person which would make them *feel* supported and better protected:

> **Polly (youth work):** I used to hope for a way into reach someone to make a point of contact and to show a connection to someone um, and you don't know what you're doing when you just do a little, a little sign of trying to help someone do something that actually means something to them

Much of this also chimes with what the young people had to say about support, and the need for someone to be there for them. Someone they could call on when they were in need, but also someone who was there because they wanted to be.

Furthermore, what can also be seen in what Cathy has to say, aligning somewhat with the young people's accounts, is that this support needs to replace or provide that which is being attained, or the need that is being met, through the sexually exploitative relationships and encounters. Many of the professionals considered that where there is grooming and a sexually exploitative relationship, there must be a counter-relationship and a sustained attention to a young person and their needs. Many spoke of the value and importance of outreach or detached workers – those who are able to meet a young person outside of formal service hours – because they provided a form of informal and responsive support for young people that they (the participants) are not able to give in their particular occupational capacity. 'Outreach' also invokes the notion of meeting young people in their own spaces – of 'going the extra mile' spatially and metaphorically, and so meeting them on their own terms, in ways that the majority of participants also felt was outside of their professional role. All the professionals spoke of the important role their relationship with a young person plays in any work they may be able to do with them. They considered that the young people they come across, who may be involved in sexually exploitative situations and relationships, can be difficult to engage and to work with. As Cathy and Faye note below:

> **Cathy (fostering):** a young person can only be helped when they want to, um you know with the best will in the world and lots and lots and lots of training it is very hard to help someone who doesn't want to be helped

> **Faye (third sector):** she was *massively vulnerable*. Um, because I don't think she had any sense of, uh, of that herself or *I don't think she would ever admit it*, she certainly wouldn't admit it and it didn't give you anything to work with

Many of the professionals considered that the difficulties experienced in engaging young people were likely to be related to their negative experiences of care, in which they had a mistrust of services and of adults more generally (see Clutton and Coles, 2007; also Melrose et al, 1999; Scott and Skidmore, 2006). Participants spoke frequently of the difficulties some young people have in engaging with them. They spoke of how young people need to have someone to whom they can expose their vulnerability, people they can trust, and people they can ask for help. In this way, a young person admitting they need help and their *wanting* to be helped by professionals was talked about as only possible through developing a trusting relationship. As Faye goes on to explain:

Faye (third sector): there was a slight sense of that I felt where they had to hold it together otherwise, what else where they going to do because they had to get, get through this evening, so if they dropped their *guard* and made themselves vulnerable with *you* and then, they had to pick themselves up and go out doing what they were doing, so, they were never going to do that, and generally they didn't, they would you'd build that relationship and they'd *know* you and they'd clock you *that evening* and then slowly they'd start to come into the centre and then you'd start to have conversations with them

As Sennett (2003: 118–19) argues, 'trust ... begins at the moment the protégée freely asks for help'. Relationships are vital to any work because they are the means of generating the trust needed for young people to begin to *want* help; and it is this which is the only way they can be helped. It is this that underpins what both the professionals and young people had to say about relationships. As Max explains:

Max (children's residential care): It's building good positive relationships with young people and that being beneficial in and of itself

The professionals' accounts concur with much of the literature, which emphasises the importance of the relationships young people have with professionals for any intervention to have meaning (see Clutton and Coles, 2007; O'Neill, 2001; Pearce et al, 2002). The importance of more open-ended relationships, and of outreach and advocacy, is a point well noted within the literature (see O'Neill, 2001, Hester and Westmarland, 2004; Kerrigan-Lebloch and King, 2006; Clutton and Coles, 2007; Pearce 2009). Yet there are few who occupy roles that can provide such a level of support, and if they do, they are most often time-restricted – as if the term 'intensive' must necessarily be preceded by 'short-term'. While the development of these relationships was seen as integral to their work with young people, participants spoke of their frustrations that they did not have time or the capacity to develop them. Those professionals who did not anticipate developing long-term relationships as part of their occupational remit, for example those working in policing or healthcare, spoke of frustrations about the lack of time to give to young people to facilitate a relationship that would enable them to disclose sensitive details about their circumstances. Other's spoke of having longer-term contact with young people, but acknowledged there was no meaningful relationship there with the young person. All considered that administrative routines and bureaucratic arrangements worked against their being able to provide the sorts of responsive bespoke support needed by young people (see Wastell et al, 2010). As Dave relates:

> **Dave (fostering):** but how often do we give people enough time with children, enough time, to sit with them *long* enough, to try and understand it, because sometimes they wouldn't understand it themselves

If the professionals are to have insight into the problem, and know how to help a young person, they need trusting relationships in which young people can share their experiences. This mirrors the young people's perspectives on relationships and trust. They too emphasised the importance of trust with those tasked to help them in order to disclose their experiences. They too emphasised the importance of time so that professionals could begin to grasp their perspectives more fully. As Dave says, there is a need for both parties to understand a young person's experiences, something that can be co-established between professional and young person. Relatedly, the professionals talked about there being a root to the problem. They spoke of the necessity to 'get to the bottom of things', to establish the reasons why they might be doing the things they are doing.

> **Carla (children's residential care):** *surely* we should be able to do that, you know like have one on one sessions, and not just listening and sitting there like I'll listen you tell me all your problems 'cos sometimes kids don't want to talk, you've got to try and get it out of them, but we're not allowed to ask questions, we're not allowed to ask question because we're, kind of pulling out stuff which, one, well the main reason I think is because we're, we'll like, make them think about all that stuff and bring all that up, which they might have suppressed, and then might not be able to deal with the consequences, but, to me that's better than just letting it go, and leaving it

As with other public service professionals, Carla believes there is some causal pattern or problem diagnosis that will get to the root of the matter, and that hearing the young person talk about 'it' is the way to revealing and dealing with the problem (see Winter, 2010). This assumption was shared by the young people who all invoked the critical nature of 'talk' within a relationship of high trust and low criticism. Carla speaks directly to Danny's frustrations, seen near the beginning of this chapter, of feeling that young people are overseen, that the interest from practitioners and other professionals is superficial, and there is no real concern to find out what a young person is dealing with. Carla relays a frustration that she can do nothing but this in her professional capacity.

"Opening up young people's world's a little bit": self-esteem and agency

The importance of these relationships comes through in another way from the professionals. Many of the professionals spoke of the need for young people to make 'good' and 'safe' choices to protect themselves. Yet underpinning what they had to say about this is the need for young people to know there *are* other ways of responding to their needs and that there *are* different ways of having relationships:

> **Faye (third sector):** I also feel it's about being really positive and building on their self-esteem [pause] where they feel, today, someone noticed me, I've got potential. I *do* think there's a sense of you can work around and there's all these other I think you've got to do both I mean if someone wants to leave a negative unhealthy relationship they need support to do that but that's not particularly our role or our expertise but we try and and do all the other things like give them the confidence to broaden their life out and have more than just this one sort of unhealthy relationship their life revolves around so we're like oh look you can do this and this and this and this, and you and you *can* do this and here we can help you to do this, that kind of thing can make their relationship seem much smaller in their eyes, and the rest of the world seem bigger, and then they might just choose to probably not even be with that person anymore because actually they've outgrown it and they've come back into their own and, feel that they can do positive things with their lives

Educating young people on ways to stay safe and helping them to make safe choices are key elements in the prevention and intervention agenda for child sexual exploitation policy (see WAG, 2011). The professionals' accounts support this, but provide some further context. They suggested that young people need to *know* they have choices, not just be told those choices are there, if they are to make changes to their lives. Moreover, as can also be seen in what Faye has to say, many of the professionals linked these choices to young people's sense of agency and self-worth. They spoke of young people needing to know "they deserve better", "to know that they can make choices", "that they can impose rules in relationships, not just have rules imposed on them". Many related this to the need to change young people's (negative) perceptions of themselves. They spoke of the importance of building up young people's confidence, and of 'instilling a sense of self-worth'. This is again similar in some ways to what the young people had to say about solutions. They spoke of how they found it helpful to hear different perspectives on their situations, and to know that things don't have to be the way they are. Yet an observation in the young people's accounts that the professionals in some ways also made is that the relational context to these conversations seems to make the difference. Tellingly, Faye makes the point, as did several participants, about the importance of young people 'being noticed' by someone, and the connection between this, young people's self-esteem and the choices they made. As suggested above, it is the trusting relationship, between the young person and the adult helping them, which provides meaning and makes the difference for the young person (see also Winter, 2010).

Sennett (2003) writes about the ways in which seeing and being seen go to the heart of respectful relations of care and welfare. He also argues that the social relationship between carer and cared for is a particular kind when the relationship is a professional one. It is not the same as friendship, and neither can it directly replace familial relationships. It is one which by its own nature requires a combination of closeness and distance, compassion and reserve, if it is to allow the care receiver and caregiver to arrive at anything like mutual respect. Mismanaged, such caring relationships can leave people feeling that they are defined almost solely according to their need(s). Alternatively, if the relationship strays into compassion and sentimentality this may similarly demean. Yet there is a difficulty here. As noted previously, the young people did not tend to speak (as Sennett does) of reserve or distance as positive qualities within the professional caring relationship. They wanted those relationships to be close, personal and compassionate, and felt unacknowledged to the degree that this did not happen. But the difficulty then is that when the state acts in loco parentis, professionals operating in this context cannot somehow fulfil that role in the way that they might as parents. They must, in short, be professional and maintain boundaries. This is similar for professionals who consider that vital parental support and care for a young person is absent, a point that Matthew alludes to:

> **Matthew (youth work):** the ones you really do sort of have an affinity with, you want to protect them so much it's like this, sort of, you almost become a surrogate father to them, because again you're um, I'm not making any correlation between the fact that the father or father figure is absent in terms of their behaviour, but they do become very, they do sort of try to hug you, and you just have to put your hand on their forehead and sort of push them away and go um just make a joke out of it, and say look, no touching, not hugging, that's not allowed, and make a joke out of it

While the difficulties negotiating care relationships spoken of by the professionals were typically more than just the occupational restrictions on physical touch (see Rees and Pithouse, 2008), the point to note with regards the above extract, is that there are of course different boundaries to the relationships caring professionals can provide, to those found in friendship or family. Indeed, not every young person is one that professionals have an 'affinity with' as Matthew puts it. Participants often spoke of 'being professional' as also having to work with young people they did not much like or get on with, yet who still required their care and commitment. However, something like family and friendship is what the young people spoke of as needing and wanting – especially when they were younger – even if in their view they did not so much need it now. The professionals too recognised this elemental need and there is much in what they had to say about responding to the problem that was consistent with what young people reported. However, as has been noted in an earlier chapter, the professionals identified time, administrative constraints and professional boundaries as necessarily curtailing their ability to provide the sorts of care that they might otherwise have wished to give (see Broadhurst et al, 2010). There is then an awkwardness if not paradox in the way that policy and practice frameworks direct work on prevention in regard to educating children and young people about healthy relationships (see WAG, 2011). Aside from the difficulties in establishing what these may look like, the accounts considered here suggest that there is not always much that is healthy about the official 'care' relationships young people have. Young people in care may not have family or friendship networks around them to care for them in the taken-for-granted ways that many of their peers do – and can be solely reliant on professionals tasked to help them to provide this. These relationships are likely to also be the very models of relationships that young people look to (see Coy, 2008).

Safeguarding and supporting young people

There are additional problems managing care relationships that the professionals described, and which are more particular when supporting sexually exploited young people. The demarcation of all victims up to the age of 18 as *children* risks homogenising identities, positioning those involved as child victims and as such non-agentic dependents (Piper, 2000). No one can reasonably deny that the needs and capabilities of a 17-year-old, the responses required and ways to best support such a person, are likely to be very different from those that apply to, say, a 12-year-old (see Pearce, 2010). As Piper (2000) argues, the children's rights agenda positions children and young people as agentic and autonomous, whereas issues of welfare and safeguarding fit more readily with an understanding of children as innocent and sexually unknowing, undeveloped and in need of protection. Child sexual exploitation fits within the latter and directs solutions towards child protection, which can be problematic when responding to the needs of young people in a number of ways. As Pearce (2010) argues, current safeguarding and social care work with young people are mostly designed for work with younger children, and their families, to provide protection within the home. In this way, the urgency of finding resources for young people involved in exchanging sex, who are demonstrably agentic, difficult to work with, do not accept help and claim they are choosing to do what they do 'diminishes in the face of cases of younger children that more closely resemble traditional child abuse' (Phoenix, 2010: 37). This is something the professionals were only too aware of and it presented them with a dilemma they found difficult to manage:

> **Nick (social work):** you are firefighting all the time trying to look for the worse cases [pause] in realism they [professionals making referrals] are right when they say these cases need to be looked into, but the sheer amount of work we have and the resources and the time mean it's not possible

Moreover, young people's risk and need of support, although very real and very urgent, when placed against the needs of younger children within families, in resource-stressed and sparse services, are unlikely to be prioritised (see Pearce, 2010; also Pithouse, 2008). Many of the professionals spoke of the difficulties they faced getting young people to be seen and prioritised as in need of support. While many emphasised young people's childlikeness and child status at times, they also spoke of having to do so, having to present young people in this way, in order for others to take their concerns seriously. Many spoke of the importance of the risk assessment framework in this context, not because it helped them to *assess or reveal* a young person's risk level, but because it provided the means to *justify* their concerns about a young person. Furthermore, they spoke of the difficulties with finding support and resources to direct towards the young people they had concerns about. Regardless of how they conceptualised the problem, all the professionals spoke of the difficulties working with young people because those they come across reject help, may not see themselves as vulnerable or at risk, may not want to be helped and may not cooperate with services trying to help them. Supporting and working with young people involved in sexual exploitation can require time and cost resources that professionals do not have. Under such circumstances, the professionals spoke of how their responses tended to be directed towards those 'worst cases', which by their very nature more obviously required and so justified protective measures. Measures which, although considered necessary, were spoken of by many of the professionals as not actually addressing the problem:

> **Annette (third sector):** I think because of the drugs I think that she was she was using more and more, I think it could very well have got to the stage where she *needed* to do what she was doing to get the money to fund the drugs. I think that would have happened quite quickly and I also feel that, you know, you, the men that she was involved with I think very clearly obviously no violence had been used up until then but that's not to say that there wouldn't have been, once they got her to the point where they felt confident enough to go down that route then maybe she wouldn't have any choice, *anymore*, you know, I think she was probably not *far off* [pause] getting to the stage where she probably, would feel that she didn't have much more choice, but then of course the police stepped in housing had stepped in everybody had stepped *in*, and she was taken

immediately out of that situation but she it wasn't what she wanted, and she was doing everything in her *power* to get back to, being able to do it again

Annette conveys a similar awareness of the short-termism of protection shown in the young people's accounts. As noted earlier, the young people spoke of the ways in which protective responses could actually feed into and exacerbate their problems. They felt that professionals too often focus on the surface of the problem and seldom address or even really see the issues that young people face. The dilemma the professionals are presented with, as Annette suggests, is the conflict between respecting the rights of the young person and protecting their best interests (see also Banks, 2004). Yet as noted above, young people are likely to come to the attention of services when their need is so great that the sorts of urgent responses spoken of by Annette are unavoidable. Young people with complex needs and who appear to refuse help do not fit easily within conceptions of vulnerability. This can leave their vulnerability and risk hidden to the professionals they variously come into contact with. This is not to say that professionals do not recognise that there are underlying issues to the problem that invariably need to be addressed. But difficulties arise when the conception of the problem does not easily enable professionals to acknowledge young people's agency. Yet, to fail to do so, to fail to see the problem as a young person sees it, is to risk misunderstanding their needs and vulnerability (see also O'Neill, 2001; Coy, 2008). This is a point ably grasped by Luke:

> **Luke (alternative education):** I suppose an adult you know you would always be told that they were able to make their own decision and you could say that young people aren't capable of making that decision, but then I would say that if you discount the [pause] you know to change a young person you have to help them to make a choice, so if you don't value the decision you know not valuing it in a positive way but if you don't take into account that they have made the choice to do what they have done, it's very difficult to reverse it [pause] um so it's about understanding the choices they have made, and working out what the problems are

The professionals' accounts strongly suggested that there are difficulties acknowledging young people's agency within a conceptualisation of the problem which assumes their lack of it. Yet acknowledging young people's agency and their choices was talked about by the professionals as essential to understanding and responding to any underlying needs and difficulties. In addition, getting to the root of the problem necessarily involves working with a young person and recognising them as an active subject within their own care (see Sennett, 2003: 118). This was an important aspect underpinning what the young people had to say about any worthwhile response to their problems. This was partly because when care took the form of being watched over and monitored, the effect could be an unwelcome sense of objectification – becoming an object of surveillance – and the diminishing sense of being properly seen as a person whom others are more fully engaged with, concerned about and prepared to look out for. It was on these terms that the young participants evaluated whether or not someone – anyone, those who exploit, as well as those tasked to care for them – could really provide the help they needed. The solutions spoken of by both professionals and young people centred on the quality of relationships with family, adults and those tasked to care for them. Yet a lack of resources to address such diffuse needs and difficulties inevitably directs responses to the immediate problem, narrowly conceived, which means putting the views of the young person second to their protection (see Leeson, 2007). While trusting relationships were considered by all participants to be essential to any aspect of prevention and intervention, 'trust' can sit awkwardly within the relationship between clients and professionals. This was felt by the young people to be especially so around issues of disclosure and confidentiality, which are essential to gaining evidence and information for professionals in order to do the work of safeguarding, but can be experienced by a young person as exposing and intrusive, making them too visible too quickly to others they don't properly know. It can compound their feeling as 'object', of interest only because of their need. This leads to a final point about the difficulties for professionals and is aptly represented in Kevin's telling statement:

> **Kevin (policing):** We are trying to safeguard children who are absolutely positively convinced that they don't need safeguarding

The problem is that professionals are tasked to respond to the needs of young people, who need more than safeguarding responses made under a policy directive to protect children. Young people are not children, or rather they are not quite children, not altogether children, not children for very much longer. If the matter were clear cut there would be less difficulty. All the young people we have heard from considered that they needed and wanted help. They all felt that there had been times when they had not got that help, when they felt ignored, and they tried to manage and cope as best they could under those circumstances, often in ways which compounded the problems they were facing. These difficulties and vulnerabilities were seen and taken advantage of by others, in ways which involved the young people exchanging and being exploited for sex, doing so because this seemed to be expected or in order to meet their needs in some way (O'Connell Davidson, 2005). There is then something also telling in what Annette says, below:

> **Annette (third sector):** I think you know we very clearly got to the point, where there was *very* little more that we could do, because she *knew* exactly what she was doing and she was making the choice to do it [pause] um and I think she, she was a victim of circumstances right probably from being a little girl she was, you know had led her to that point

While there are no 'solutions' that might eradicate the problem as such, there is an urgent need to direct resources towards the needs of young people to enable professionals to see, support and work with them as young people. When responses are designed for children, they are unlikely to be helpful for young people, in the longer term at least. So here I return to my argument that there is a need to look to the wider context of sexual exploitation, to understand the links between the problem, and vulnerability and risk (see also Pearce et al, 2002; Coy, 2008). An important part of this, as can be seen in what Annette conveys, a point made by all participants, is that there is a need to also look to the extent, relevance and accessibility of support that is given to vulnerable children, because an important part of any solution rests in the quality and design of preventative engagement.

Responding to child sexual exploitation

The young people considered that the *real* problems were the underlying vulnerabilities which make 'being taken advantage of in a sexual way' possible; and it is *this* which forms the problem which needs to be addressed. This was something which the young people felt was not always recognised by those trying to help them because adults tended to focus more on their behaviour. Child sexual exploitation is a problem that is preventable. Yet more than that, and significantly from the perspectives of the young people interviewed, prevention *is* the solution to the problem. Sexual exploitation was considered to be something that doesn't have to happen at all. According to the young people in this study the *real* problem lies with those issues and unmet needs that make being taken advantage of possible. Feeling vulnerable, uncertain, powerless, overlooked and unseen, ignored, misunderstood and without help – these were the problems that, for them, needed solving. The young people did not typically invoke a need for some specific help such as money, housing, help with addiction, albeit such issues lay behind their sexual exploitation. This is not to suggest they did not want help in these areas, but rather their focus was on relationships – more specifically, care relationships in which they could feel seen, acknowledged and heard; in which they could feel recognised as people first and where the work by professionals in relation to their needs came second.

As I have considered, young people alluded to countervailing categories of object/subject experiences whereby they recognised they were acknowledged and 'cared for', or felt in some ways as subject, by *those abusing them*. Meanwhile they also described feelings in many ways viewed as 'objects' of concern by those officially charged with their care who cannot always see or meet their relational needs. The multitude of professionals involved in the young people's lives, mobilised only because of their need for protection, meant the young people were *of concern*. Yet, perversely, the relationships with some professionals and carers, driven by the requirements of child protection, could compound those difficulties and issues due to a lack of opportunity for young people to feel they were of concern for reasons other than their 'neediness'. Sennett (2003) writes about how feeling and being an active subject in one's care is to be acknowledged as an individual who is seen as more than a person in need of help *and* it is also to feel a sense of control over the care itself. It is within these care relationships that the troubled sense of agency described by the young people in previous chapters began to change. Relationships are not just essential because they provide the means for getting the work done. They are the work. Autonomy requires reciprocal relationships (see Sennett, 2003). As Berger (2013: 177) considers, in order to feel recognised as a person (and not a problem, or category, or case) there must be some reciprocity or interdependency – '[b]etween people there is no such thing as unilateral one way knowledge'. By having someone there to acknowledge them, by feeling heard and seen, listened to and understood, the young people acquired a degree of security, stability and a sense of their own agency and control, which enabled them to believe they could 'move on' and to experience change as something positive. Honneth's (2014) theory of recognition can be summarised thus: the 'I' is dependent on a sense of 'we'. It is only through relationships and groups, shared norms, practices and beliefs that identity and a sense of 'I' can be realised, established and maintained. Which draws our attention to the shared norms within care as a statutory responsibility on one level, and to those in the wider relationships and social contexts within which young people operate and live.

Another key point is that there is no opportunity to conceive of prevention or intervention in these terms within a policy framework organised around the construct of 'children' and the limiting discourse of 'grooming'. 'Child sexual exploitation' necessarily directs practice to child protection – the sharp end of social work and which, on its own, may not respond to the problem in the ways the participants here considered to be helpful. The problem of sexual exploitation can therefore become circular, in a number of ways. To repeat, the young people spoke of sexual exploitation as a problem of people taking advantage of their vulnerabilities, their unmet needs and issues, their ways of coping. It cannot be bracketed as some separable and distinct problem from these other 'things going on' in their lives. Their accounts suggest a lack of recognition among those tasked to help them, of the contribution of these unmet needs to the problem. This can leave young people unnoticed by those who might help, or focus attention on the young person and their behaviours leaving them feeling unrecognised as a person, with their needs and vulnerable circumstances unrecognised too. In this way, responses can inform the very problem they are attempting to disrupt. Framed solely as child protection, it can be difficult for professionals to respond in the ways that the young people spoke of wanting and needing (see Phoenix, 2002, 2010; Pearce, 2009). Their accounts suggest that practices of care in which priority is given to investigation and minimising danger rather than looking to promote aspects of wellbeing (Daniel, 2010: 235) form part of and contribute to the problem itself. This echoes concerns within the literature and research, which have shown that the use of 'protective' measures, such as secure units, can be unsuccessful in making any long-term differences for young people (see for example Creegan et al, 2005; Clutton and Coles, 2007; Beckett, 2011). O'Neill (2001) has argued that defining young people as victims of abuse in need of protection does not necessarily create better outcomes for them, and they may become subject to forms of protection that are perceived as punitive in their effect. 'Protection', instigated as a sole response, misunderstands the problem as the young people see it and may only provide a short-term resolution, while serving to make young people more vulnerable.

The focus on grooming deflects attention from wider socioeconomic structures that cause adversity (Day, 2009), while also directing practice to see the needs and wishes of an individual young person as *secondary* to their protection (see Warrington, 2010). When a young person's victim status depends on their being without agency, a difficulty arises in positioning young people as 'capable' within their own care. Protective responses are legitimated by discourses of childhood and grooming; and also become *necessary*, while ignoring their role in the creation of the problem, as the young people and professionals see it. Allowing for an understanding of 'conditions of consent' (see Pitts, 1997) would redirect attention to young people's sense of agency – and would also open up the possibility of responses that recognise it, such as harm reduction and work with young people to mitigate harm (see Hickle and Hallett, 2016). There is an urgent need to consider young people's own understandings of their situations in order to ensure that responses can be directed towards taking into account the help that young people feel they need. Repositioning sexual exploitation as abuse through exchanging sex brings attention to the matter of unmet needs, which in turn brings attention to the need for multiple responses to address the complex underlying issues underpinning such relationships and encounters (see also Hester and Westmarland, 2004; Kerrigan-Lebloch and King, 2006; Melrose and Pearce, 2013; Hickle and Hallett, 2016). This allows for a consideration of responses that extend far more widely than individual care relationships, or even care systems, taking into account the wider socioeconomic context for sexual exploitation.

Conclusion: child sexual exploitation – agency, abuse and exchange

In the introduction, this book was defined as an exploration of the problem of child sexual exploitation from the viewpoints of young people with experiences of it, and of those charged with their support and protection. It was indicated then, and will be clear by now, that this issue extends outwards into a series of other related problems, most obviously the multiple and concatenating difficulties experienced by young people that make them vulnerable, and which run alongside their experience of sexual exploitation. Then there are the challenges experienced by professionals in their attempts to respond to young people identified in this way – dilemmas of practice, some (not all) openly acknowledged. Then there are the problems arising from the way in which 'child sexual exploitation' as a social problem is constructed and articulated in policy and practice frameworks. Given which, and in bringing the discussion to a close, there will now be a consolidating discussion of the data, analysis and key arguments that have featured throughout.

Fundamentally, there are problems arising from the way in which child sexual exploitation is conceptualised within current policy frameworks. Child sexual exploitation is not only a problem per se but is also, in itself, problematic in terms of definition. This is particularly so in respect of the way in which the problem is framed and defined as the grooming of children by predatory adults. It has been argued that this conceptualisation is narrow and obfuscating, inhibiting a fuller understanding of young people's experiences, which, in turn, limits what it is that professionals can see and are able to do when faced with a young person in need. This adds support to the argument that there is an urgent need for policy and practice frameworks to explicitly recognise those involved in the exchange of sex outside of grooming in order to acknowledge and promote much-needed support for young people in these sorts of difficulties (see Pearce et al, 2002; Phoenix, 2002; Moore, 2006; Pearce, 2010; Melrose, 2012). Responses to the problem need to acknowledge and address the reasons that underpin why it is that some young people may be 'groomed', or feel that the exchange of sex is expected or inevitable, and is the best or 'least worst' option.

Given the above, it is argued that the current policy framework, so explicit in its reference to the grooming of children by adults, is problematic for professionals in four ways. First, it oversimplifies, creating too narrow a definition. The current conception of CSE risks collapsing varied experiences into a singular category of grooming, yet this model does not fully measure up to the problem as participants described it (see also Day, 2009; O'Connell Davidson, 2005). The accounts given by the young people in this study revealed how they also exchange sex to meet needs. They exchange sex when they feel it is expected. They can be aware of their exploitation. They can, and do, within constrained and limited choices, choose to exchange sex to meet those needs (see also Pitts, 1997; Pearce et al, 2002; Moore, 2006). To say this is not to underplay or dilute the concern we should feel about any young person in such circumstances; it is instead to see young people's experience of sexually exploitative relationships for what they are.

Second, the relatively narrow definition within policy does not allow professionals to easily understand the complexity and variety of child sexual exploitation and so recognise it. As shown earlier, the professionals sometimes displayed uncertainty about the problem itself – one related to confusion about when or whether their concerns about a young person meet the definition in policy and thereby require a safeguarding response. Indeed, they may not come across grooming, but they may well encounter young people exchanging sex who they consider to be sexually exploited. As suggested earlier, it is not so much that the problem is hidden and not easily visible, it is rather that the definition of the problem within policy frameworks constructs a slim aperture through which to look out from. The instances of CSE that professionals perceive and come across need a bigger lens in order to capture and interpret the problem (see Pearce, 2009). Counterintuitively, the highly bounded nature of policy definitions appears to yield vagueness rather than precision, making child sexual exploitation difficult to identify. If the problem is deemed officially as one of grooming (from an adult male), and the preventative focus is on educating young people about healthy relationships, then the variability and complexity of sexual exploitation is not by any means made easy to see.

Third, the instances of CSE that professionals are likely to encounter and need to perceive require a wider and more nuanced lens for it to be interpreted and understood as such. The emphasis on grooming, as the coercion of children by *adults*, and in which children do not recognise their exploitation, frames an understanding of the problem as that of child victim and adult perpetrator, obscuring the complexities of sexually exploitative relationships for young people, and can lead

144

to a (false) understanding that what professionals should expect to see is someone who fits some notion of innocence and vulnerability (see Williams 2010). This point is ably intimated by Louisa:

> **Louisa (social work):** I don't know I suppose when I think about the word sexual exploitation a lot of what comes to my mind is what uh kind of cities and paedophile rings and um, child trafficking, whereas in my in my experience in work that isn't really what it's been like [pause] um I suppose in my experience it's been a, a bit more kind of about the sexual abuse, and um you know a young person being used and people taking advantage of them ... I don't know like sometimes using the language like using the language of perpetrator, can bring with it uh, a lot of people automatically associate a lot of things to that [pause] rather than, I suppose you can make judgements about a situation that's maybe what I'm trying to say, and you can maybe make judgements about a victim and judgements about a perpetrator because of the language, rather than being able to analyse it fresh [pause] and seeing everything that's going on

Louisa explains something of the challenge for professionals tasked to identify this problem. 'Child sexual exploitation', underpinned as it is by the grooming discourse, invites us to see the problem as organised groups of adult men exploiting children (see Pearce, 2010; Melrose, 2010). This no doubt occurs, indeed this book opened with reference to a spate of high profile convictions in 2012–14 that match this model well. However, the difficulty for many professionals is that the instances of concern that they come across day-to-day are, more often, as Louisa explains in the very same words as the young participants, "young people being used" and "taken advantage of", in multiple and often routine ways, and some distance from notions of organised gangs of predatory males. This creates two issues: how to find ways to justify resources and time to respond to these instances, and the difficulties non-specialist professionals have in seeing these as sexual exploitation at all (see also Phoenix, 2010). As Kelly et al, observe:

> We regard it as dangerous to create classifications of sexual abuse which are constructed as mutually exclusive categories. Whilst conceptualisation enables an increasing recognition of the various forms of sexual abuse, the

contexts they occur in and the consequences they have, we
need to bear in mind that these are analytical categories,
and the boundaries created are often artificial ... We must
beware the danger of constructing the very problem we are
supposed to be investigating – in other words do we only
find what we expect to see? (Kelly et al, 1995: 14)

The professionals in this study understood that child sexual exploitation
sits in a wider context of problems and the young people insisted this
too, which leads to the fourth point. The focus on grooming makes
it difficult for professionals to acknowledge and respond to some
of the wider issues surrounding the exchange of sex. Even when
sexual exploitation does take the form of grooming, it is invariably
underpinned by problems and vulnerabilities in the lives of young
people, the 'things going on' in their lives – that recurrent, revealing, yet
inexact phrase used by the young participants, which captures this often
turbulent and unhappy background. These need to be acknowledged
if professionals are going to be able to identify the problem when it
occurs. As the young people often alluded to, as did Louisa above,
professionals need to look beyond the presenting circumstances and
initial perceptions of young people in order to see all those 'things
going on'. It is in exploring this poorly illuminated and overlooked
background that professionals may be best enabled to understand and
identify that a young person is being sexually exploited. Finally, with
such a strong emphasis on the manipulation and coercion of children by
adults, one resting on normative conceptions of children as dependent,
innocent and with a lack of agency, 'young people' do not easily fit
within this conception. Furthermore, when the problem itself involves
young people who appear to put themselves in risky situations, or
who consider it their choice to exchange sex, the limited space for
professionals to acknowledge and make sense of this can mean that
the needs and the reasons underpinning these young people's sexual
exploitation can be ignored – leaving them further vulnerable. This
leads on to the next key point.

Agency, choice, consent

Agency, responsibility, blame, and conceptions of vulnerability are
integral to the evolution and conceptualisation of this problem. As I
have considered, child sexual exploitation 'exists' within policy and
practice as a social care issue because it is *child* sexual exploitation:
the corollary being that 'child sexual exploitation' exists because a

distinction between 'adults' and 'children' within policy has been made (Jeffreys, 2000). This recent distinction between adults and children involved in prostitution, while made with reference to age, 'rights' and distinct sets of entitlements to protection and support, is set within a discursive framework that is intrinsically bound to primary conceptions of childhood (Melrose, 2010). Brown (2004: 345), in her study exploring the establishment and development of categories of child abuse, argues that 'the assumptions of comprehension and choice on the part of the child have been instrumental in excluding child prostitution from being encompassed in definitions of child abuse'. Necessarily thereby, the very existence of the problem as an official category of concern is one which depends on and is premised on this conception. As Piper (2000: 27) argues, 'the public image of the child, which has served both to encourage and justify social policy, is of an "unsexualised" person who is vulnerable, weak and innocent'.

As discussed in Chapter One, an enduring feature of historical and contemporary representations of child sexual exploitation, and of the young people caught up in it, has been, in one way or another, to locate the problem as occurring within deviant individuals; allowing for the problem to be positioned away from the family, home, society and its institutions, and so a problem not *with* society but *for* it. The focus on the individual has become all pervasive, where the problems within society are frequently portrayed as being caused by individuals themselves and not wider structural inequalities (Phoenix, 2010). These neoliberalist values are also reflected in policies and practice which over the last 30 years or so have been increasingly designed so that 'only those who behave will receive support and encouragement' (Pearce 2007: 207). Set in this context, as Doezema (1998) considers, the discourse around sexual exploitation sets a moralistic framework that categorises people as either guilty or innocent, based on perceptions about their agency, their responsibility, their level of choice. O'Connell Davidson and Anderson (2006: 22) continue this point and warn that this creates 'moral hierarchies' in which those who are exploited can be perceived as 'deserving... less deserving... and undeserving' of support or sympathy depending on perceptions of their competency and vulnerability.

In this way, the discursive construction of child sexual exploitation, positioned heavily as grooming, and underpinned by ideologies of childhood, can exclude and bring particular problems for young people. On the face of it, this should not be so. As outlined previously, 'young people', within policy and within society, are still considered to be children, posited as all those aged up to 18 years. By virtue of this age related category, young people hold a specific set of welfare and social rights, and policy on this issue is also explicit in its reference to 'young people' and that the 'child' in child sexual exploitation applies to all those aged up to 18. Furthermore, in Wales for example, the risk assessment framework includes a referral protocol for those aged up to 21 who can be classed as 'vulnerable young adults' (see WAG, 2011: 29–30). In this way policy could not be clearer in claiming that sexual exploitation affects all children, including young people. The difficulty for 'young people', as a category of persons and those occupying it, is that they are not safely ensconced within a conception of childhood. Young people are a 'grey area' between the normative, seemingly distinct black and white categories of adulthood and childhood; it is the boundary state, the time of transition, the time of *becoming* adult; and a period which can be stretched in either direction (Lee, 2001; Wyn and White, 1997). They can be *like* adults. 'Young people' have responsibilities, and can be considered able to consent to adult experiences. As such, and as Dean (1997) argues, they are both object and subject of the welfare state, their responsibilities are as ambiguous as their rights. They can be deemed and held accountable in many areas of social and welfare related policy (Dean, 1997). O'Connell Davidson (2001: 59) refers to Hoffman's distinction between 'victims' and 'victimhoods'; the latter referring to a pathology within which certain groups are seen by others (and may see themselves) as objects, without the capacity to defend their own interests. While this can elicit responses to pain and suffering, it can serve to minimise the harm that occurs to those who are 'socially imagined as full subjects'. In addition, as Phoenix (2010: 37) argues, 'if sex, sexual exchanges and consuming sex is normalised within society', 'young people', who are accepted as part consumer and part responsible citizen, can be perceived as being less in need: the less childlike the child, the less harm their involvement in the exchange of sex can be perceived to be, or the less at risk, or victim–like they seem to be. Arguably, it is for these reasons that the discourse of 'child sexual exploitation' is also one which particularly serves to exclude young males, transgendered and transsexual young people, and those observed to be 'streetwise' or 'troublesome' (Lillywhite and Skidmore, 2006; Melrose, 2010). As Williams (2010: 251) suggests

> the portrayal of the weak, 'innocent', helpless victim is directly challenged by the teen the police or a would–be service provider encounters in the field. Instead of a sad–eyed victim, they confront a strong, wilful, survivor who

looks and acts quite differently from the victims portrayed
in the media.

The ambiguity and contradictions of the social category 'youth' is
thrown into sharp relief in the context of 'child sexual exploitation'
defined as something that can happen to anyone up to the age of 18.

Vulnerabilities, risks and wider problems

The findings here indicate that the problem of sexual exploitation is one
that is intrinsically connected to young people's social and emotional
worlds. The vulnerabilities and risks set out within policy guidance
as indicators of the problem, from the perspectives of the participants
in this study, *are* the problem – in that they cannot be separated out
from the sexually exploitative circumstances and relationships in which
children and young people are involved – and acknowledging this is
vital to any full understanding of the problem. In the previous chapters,
we have heard the young people speak of (child) sexual exploitation
as inseparable from the many other 'things going on' in their lives:
things such as their feelings of being without help, feeling uncared for
and unseen, their finding ways to cope that often compounded their
difficulties. From the perspectives of the young people, these 'things
going on' were the real risk and root of the problem. The professional
participants did not go so far as to suggest that a young person's
underlying vulnerabilities and risky behaviours were the problem itself,
yet they considered these to be related to the problem in such a way
that they could not be ignored. They understood there to be a 'root',
a reason or reasons, particular to a young person that needed to be
addressed. These underlying needs and vulnerabilities, spoken of by
both sets of participants, inform an understanding of sexual exploitation
that is broader than one which sees young people being groomed and
exploited for sex (see also Phoenix, 2010; Melrose, 2012). A key aspect
of this was care. 'Care' was a recurrent theme throughout the data
gathered from both sets of participants in respect of the problems and
solutions to child sexual exploitation. If the purpose of placing young
people in settings where they are overseen by professionals tasked to
care for them is to protect them from further harm by recognising
(*seeing* and *seeing to*) their needs and vulnerabilities, then at least some
young people seem to experience this attention negatively. As I have
argued elsewhere:

> not only does adult care giving and practices of child
> protection feature in the young people's accounts as being
> part of the problem, but the instigation of these practices,
> made as a response to a young person's involvement in
> sexually exploitative situations, can ignore, or miss, the
> 'real' problem of sexual exploitation as the young people
> see it, and may also serve to compound the problem which
> it is attempting to prevent and disrupt. (Hallett, 2015: 14)

A clear thread running through both sets of respondent data is that
young people can, and do, feel themselves to be in many ways 'invisible'
to those who should care for them. The sorts of attention given a
vulnerable child or young person by those with an official duty of care
can be the type of engagement that makes for further vulnerability
if that intervention is experienced as 'blotting out their individuality
and subjectivity' (O'Connell Davidson, 2005: 55). Yet it can be very
difficult for professionals to provide the sorts of care, attention and
affection that all children and young people (or in fact all individuals)
need. These professionals considered that they and other professionals
like them, struggle to meet the needs of the children and young people
they are working with. This can leave young people looking for the
sorts of caring supportive relationships that any person needs, and which
in the absence of a positive nurturing other makes them vulnerable
to people who might exploit them for sex. These young people felt
powerless, uncared for, and without help or attention. Under such
circumstances 'sexual exploitation' can be an answer of sorts, a form
of 'help' and recognition of *some* form from *someone*.

As argued in the previous chapter, it was within often contradictory
and countervailing categories of a subject/object experience that sexual
exploitation was made sense of by the young people participating in
this study. The missing ingredient in the professionals' accounts is the
consideration of young people's subject experiences. A young person
is understood to be vulnerable because they have many experiences in
which they are denied as subjects – through their lack of meaningful
reciprocal relationships, their lack of place and home and in their
status as objects of care. Yet, in the professionals' talk about risk, they
too deny young people as real subjective actors, arguably because,
as discussed throughout, young people do not 'fit' easily within the
current conception of child sexual exploitation within policy. And
therein lies the contradiction and the source of some confusion.
For young people (in particular) to be visible within 'child sexual
exploitation', they cannot also be visible as active subjects. Young

people sit somewhat uncomfortably on the fringes of this issue because, to reiterate, the current discourse with its focus on grooming by adult men is connected to the notion that young people are considered unable to give informed consent in some authentic sense, because they are by definition 'children'. It follows that they must have been forced to participate (see O'Connell Davidson, 2005; Melrose, 2012). Hence the 'problem' of sexual exploitation is not linked to the sorts of vulnerabilities discussed throughout or in regard to the ways in which young people resolve or cope with them, but is limited to 'men who exploit' (Phoenix, 2002: 359).

Making sense of CSE?

We have come a long way from talking about child prostitution, with all its historical and contemporary associations. While it is not the case that I advocate a return to that terminology, there are problems with 'child sexual exploitation' that go beyond the sorts of public and professional confusion outlined within this book, and which are not limited to a lack of understanding. As I have considered, the change in terminology has brought about a change in understanding of the phenomena itself. CSE is not just a replacement term for prostitution but is representative of a paradigm shift in understanding and in the framing of the problem. Arguably the term has become so far removed from its historical roots that they are now unrecognisable, as are many of the instances of sexual exploitation experienced by children and young people which do not fit within this current conception. What, for example, of the young people whose experiences sit outside of gangs, grooming or any obvious relationship? And, more than this, how might we now connect the experiences of a child or young person in the UK with a child or young 'prostitute' in, say, Cambodia, when using the terminology of sexual exploitation in its current discursive framing?

There are many ways that young people can be sexually exploited. The accounts considered here describe brainwashing and manipulation into sexual activity, transient encounters or transactional sex when sex is the expected condition, and selling sex as a coping strategy or resource. Sexual exploitation can occur within or be legitimated through family relationships, through peer relationships, through groups or individuals. The element of exchange is what is present through all these accounts. It is this – exchange – that makes sexual exploitation particular and distinct from other forms of sexual abuse. Not only this, but it is essential to any full or rounded understanding of CSE. Acknowledging the exchange occurring within this form of sexual abuse (even when the exchange is the withdrawal of something) brings attention to and recognition of the wider context surrounding sexually exploitative relationships and encounters. It positions the vulnerabilities and unmet needs as part of the problem that require attention. More than this, exchange as a model allows space to consider and understand young people's sense of agency, and the sorts of object/subject experiences described throughout this book, without somehow denying the abuse that is occurring through these exploitative relationships and encounters. In so acknowledging, it opens up the space to recognise the sexual exploitation that occurs but which currently sits outside of the narrow parameters of CSE as defined by the grooming model. Understanding sexual exploitation as 'the sexual abuse of children and young people through the activity of exchanging sex' re-centres this as the problem, rather than the coercion or manipulation of children and young people specifically, which would also allow us to consider and connect the experiences of children and young people abused through exchanging sex globally, and also allow us to consider those wider harms and societal structures that make such abuse possible.

I hope to have provided insights which enable those seeking to work in the best interests of children and young people experiencing sexual exploitation, to understand better the reasons for children and young people's vulnerability and their often severely constrained circumstances due to which they sometimes choose or feel they have to exchange sex. It is hoped that the modest contribution the arguments in this book can make is one which helps those with similar experiences to the young people in this research. It has been my aim to provide insights that reveal the complexity of the phenomena while also providing a theoretically informed, critical contribution towards understanding what child sexual exploitation is. In so doing I have sought to avoid adding further confusion to what is already a field of some uncertainty and contestation. In illuminating something of its complexity I have attempted to challenge and enhance what is already known about the problem, and to 'speak' on behalf of those young people who are often obscured or unnoticed within policy legislation and by censorious public debate and media reports. These are those young people who, within current conceptions of the problem, are not much recognised and whose needs can be difficult for professionals to identify, recognise, prioritise and direct resources towards. These are young people who experience significant trauma, abuse and harm, and who are in need of welfare, care and support. In all this I am well aware that for some readers, as Melrose observed over a decade ago:

Acknowledging that there are some young people involved in [sexual exploitation] who have not been forced into it by an abusive adult may seem like political suicide to those who have campaigned long and hard to have these young people accepted as in need of care and protection rather than punishment. (2004: 9)

Yet, as argued throughout, the historical (and continuing) discourse around CSE means that it is *because* campaigners want to see young people in these sorts of circumstances better supported that more recent campaigns have focused on young people's lack of agency and (in)ability to consent, and hence are in clear need of intervention.[1] There has been no other way of having the conversation. Yet, as considered throughout this book, the problem of child sexual exploitation is not just one experienced by younger children. It is not just a problem of grooming, and it is not just a problem of *adults* sexually exploiting children and young people. Young people who exchange sex for money, other material goods, for support and care, because they do not have a sense of agency that means they feel able to see exchanging sex as anything other than expected, are those for whom the paradigm shift within policy to one of social care rather than criminal justice occurred. Yet these are also the young people who (according to the findings here) are still difficult to recognise and respond to within the definitions of CSE in contemporary policy. Ten years on from Melrose's statement, despite 'child sexual exploitation' now being firmly established within social care policy, despite the significant increase in professional and public awareness of 'CSE' and the continued presence of sexual exploitation within media debates, we still do not hear much of young people involved in sexually exploitative relationships and circumstances who are not in some way 'groomed'. We do not see their more complex experiences represented within more straightforward definitions of the problem within policy and practice frameworks. Young people who exhibit agency in some way are unlikely to be seen as 'real' victims or, at the very least, there is no space to even acknowledge this agency because of the risk of this judgement. We still only hear of grooming; and the fault, according to the current political narrative, lies with those who groom, and those individual practitioners and professionals who fail to notice young people's risk and are wilfully ignorant of their abuse. There the problem stops.

As does this analysis, for now. I conclude by offering the last words to one of the young participants:

People don't listen to young people do they? They need to listen more, don't they? They need to hear people like me…

Notes

[1]   See for example: www.barnardos.org.uk/get_involved/campaign/cutthemfree/remembertheyarechildren.htm

References

Adams, N., Carter, C., Carter, S., Lopez-Jones, N. and Mitchell, C. (1997) 'Demystifying child prostitution: a street view' in Barrett, D. (ed) *Child Prostitution in Britain*. London: The Children's Society (122–38).

Adey, P. (2006) 'If Mobility is Everything Then it is Nothing: Towards a Relational Politics of (Im)Mobilities'. *Mobilities*. 1, (1), 75–94.

Aitchison, P. and O'Brien, R. (1997) 'Redressing the balance: The legal context of child prostitution' in Barrett, D. (eds) *Child Prostitution in Britain*. London: The Children's Society (76–89).

Alexander, C. and Charles, G. (2009) 'Caring, Mutuality and Reciprocity in Social Worker-Client Relationships: Rethinking Principles of Practice'. *Journal of Social Work*. 9, (5), 5–22.

Arksey, H. and Knight, P. (1999) *Interviewing for Social Scientists*. London: Sage.

Ayre, P. and Barrett, D. (2000) 'Young people and prostitution: an end to the beginning?'. *Children and Society*. 14, (1), 48–59.

Banks, S. (2004) 'The dilemmas of intervention' in Roche, J., Tucker, S., Thomson, R.., and Flynn, R. (eds) *Youth and Society: Contemporary Theory, Policy and Practice* (2nd edition). London: Sage (218–26).

Barrett, D. (eds) (1997) *Child Prostitution in Britain*. London: The Children's Society.

Barry, K. (1979) *Sexual Slavery*. New York: New York University Press.

Beckett, H. (2011) *'Not a world away': The sexual exploitation of children and young people in Northern Ireland*. Belfast: Barnardo's Cymru.

Berelowitz, S., Firmin, C., Edwards, G. and Gulyurtlu., S. (2012) *"I thought I was the only one. The only one in the world" The Office of the Children's Commissioner's Inquiry into Child Sexual Exploitation In Gangs and Groups. Interim Report*. London: Office of The Children's Commissioner, England.

Berger, J. (2013) 'Recognition' in *Understanding a Photograph*. London: Penguin.

Biggs, S. (2001) 'Toward Critical Narrativity: Stories of Aging in Contemporary Social Policy'. *Journal of Aging Studies*. 15, 303–16.

Bourdieu, P. (1999) 'Understanding' in Bourdieu, P. et al. (eds) *The Weight of The World: Social Suffering in Contemporary Society*. Cambridge: Polity Press.

Bowlby, J. (1977) 'The making and breaking of affectional bonds. I. Aetiology and psychopathology in the light of attachment theory. An expanded version of the Fiftieth Maudsley Lecture, delivered before the Royal College of Psychiatrists, 19 November 1976'. *The British Journal of Psychiatry*. 130, 201–10.

Boyden, J. (2006) 'Childhood and the Policy Makers: A Comparative Perspective on the Globalization of Childhood' in James, A. and Prout, A. (eds) *Constructing and Reconstructing Childhood* (2nd edition). Abingdon, Oxon: Routledge (190–229).

Broadhurst, K., Wastell, D., White., S., Hall., C., Peckover., S., Thompson., K., Pithouse, A. and Davey, D. (2010) 'Performing 'Initial Assessment': identifying the latent conditions for error at the front-door of local authority children's services'. *British Journal of Social Work*. 40, (2), 352–70.

Brown, A. (2004) 'Mythologies and panics: twentieth century constructions of child prostitution'. *Children and Society*. 18, 344–54.

Brown, A. and Barrett, D. (2002) *Knowledge of Evil: Child Prostitution and Child Sexual Abuse in Twentieth Century*. England Devon: Willan Publishing.

Butler, I. and Drakeford, M. (2012) *Social work on trial: the Colwell inquiry and the state of welfare*. Bristol: The Policy Press.

Calder, M. (2001) 'Child prostitution: developing effective protocols'. *Child Care in Practice*. 7, (2), 98–115.

Casey, L. (2015) *Reflections on Child Sexual Exploitation*. London: Department for Communities and Local Government.

CEOP (2011) *Out of Mind, Out of Sight: Breaking Down the Barriers To Understanding Child Sexual Exploitation*. London: CEOP.

Chase, E. and Statham, J. (2005) 'Commercial and sexual exploitation of children and young people in the UK – A review'. *Child Abuse Review*. 14, (1), 4–25.

Clutton, S. and Coles, J. (2007) *Sexual Exploitation Risk Assessment Framework: a Pilot Study*. Cardiff: Barnardo's Cymru.

Clutton, S. and Coles, J. (2008) *Child Sexual Exploitation in Wales: 3 Years On*. Cardiff: Barnardo's Cymru.

Coffey, A. (1999) *The Ethnographic Self: Fieldwork and the Representation of Identity*. London: Sage.

Coffey, A. and Hall, T. (eds) (2011) *Researching Young People, volumes 1–3*. London: Sage.

Cohen, S. (2002) *Folk Devils and Moral Panics: Creation of Mods and Rockers* (3rd edition). New York: Routledge.

Coles, B. (2000) *Joined-up Youth Research, Policy and Practice: a New Agenda for Change?* Leicester: Youth Work Press.

Coles, J. (2005) *Out of Sight: Out of Mind*. Barkingside: Barnardo's.

Corteen, K. and Scraton, P. (1997) 'Prolonging "Childhood", Manufacturing "Innocence" and Regulating Sexuality' in Scraton, P. (ed) *Childhood in 'Crisis?* London: UCL Press (76–100).

Coy, M. (2008) 'Young women, local authority care and selling sex'. *British Journal of Social Work*. 38, 1408–24.

Coy, M. (2016) 'Joining the dots on sexual exploitation of children and women: A way forward for UK policy responses'. *Critical Social Policy*. 36, (4), 572–91.

Cree, V.E., Clapton, G. and Smith, M. (2012) 'The Presentation of Child Trafficking in the UK: An Old and New Moral Panic?'. *British Journal of Social Work.* (Advanced access DOI: 10.1177/0261018312457860)

Creegan, C., Scott, S. and Smith, S. (2005) *Use Of Secure Accommodation And Alternative Provisions For Sexually Exploited Young People In Scotland.* Scotland: Barnardo's Scotland.

Cusick, L. (2002) 'Youth prostitution: a literature review'. *Child Abuse Review.* 11, 230–51.

Daniel, B. (2010) 'Concepts of adversity, risk, vulnerability and resilience: a discussion in the context of the 'child protection system". *Social Policy and Society.* 9, (2), 231–41.

Daniel, P. and Ivatts, J. (1998) *Children and Social Policy.* Hampshire: Palgrave.

Davies, P. and Feldman, R. (1992) 'Prostitute Men Now' in Scambler, G., and Scambler, A. (eds) *Rethinking Prostitution: Purchasing Sex in the 1990s.* Routledge, London and New York.

Davis, N.J. (1978) 'Prostitution: Identity, Career and Legal Economic Enterprise' in Henslin, J. and Sagarin, E. (eds) *The Sociology of Sex.* New York: Schocken Books.

Day, S. (2009) 'Renewing the War on prostitution: The spectres of 'trafficking' and 'slavery". *Anthropology Today.* 25, (3), 1–3.

Dean, H. (1997) 'Underclassed or undermined? Young People and Social Citizenship' in Macdonald, R. (ed) *Youth, the 'Underclass' and Social Exclusion.* London: Routledge (55–69).

Department for Children Schools and Families (2009) *Safeguarding Children and Young People from Sexual Exploitation: Supplementary Guidance to Working Together to Safeguard Children.* London: DCSF.

Department of Health (DoH) (2000) *Safeguarding Children Involved in Prostitution.* London: DoH.

Department of Health (DoH) (2003) *Sexual Offences Act.* London: DoH.

Doezema, J. (1998) 'Forced to Choose: Beyond the Voluntary Vs Forced Prostitution Dichotomy' in Kempadoo, K. and Doezema, J. (eds) *Global Sex Workers: Rights, Resistance and Redefinition.* New York: Routledge (34–50).

Drinkwater, S., Greenwood, H. and Melrose, M. (2004) 'Young People Exploited Through Prostitution: A Literature Review' in Melrose, M. and Barrett, D. (eds) *Anchors in Floating Lives: Interventions with Young People Sexually Abused Through Prostitution.* Lyme Regis, Dorset: Russell House Publishing (23–35).

Edinburgh L. and Saewyc, E. (2008). 'A novel, intensive home-visiting intervention for runaway, sexually exploited girls.' *Journal for Specialists in Pediatric Nursing.* 14(1): 41–8.

Edwards, T. (2004) 'Sexuality' in Roche, J., Tucker, S., Thomson, R. and Flynn, R. (eds) *Youth in Society: Contemporary Theory, Policy and Practice.* London: Sage (168–76).

Ennew, J. (1986) *The Sexual Exploitation of Children*. Cambridge: Polity Press.

Faulkner, J. (2011) *The Importance of Being Innocent: Why We Worry About Children*. Australia: Cambridge University Press.

Fine, M., Weis, L., Weseen, S. and Wong, L. (2000) 'For whom? Qualitative research, Representations and Social Responsibilities' in Denzin, N.K. and Lincoln, Y.S. (eds) *Handbook of Qualitative Research*. Thousand Oaks California: Sage Publications (107–32).

Firmin, C. (2011) *This is it. This is my life...Female Voice in Violence*. Final Report. London: ROTA.

Firmin, C. (2013) 'Something Old or Something New: Do Pre-Existing Conceptualisations of Abuse Enable a Sufficient Response to Abuse in Young People's Relationships and Peer Groups?' in Melrose, M., and Pearce, J. (eds) *Critical Perspectives on Child Sexual Exploitation and Related Trafficking*. Hampshire: Palgrave Macmillan.

Foley, D., Scammel, J., and Wood, R. (2004) 'BASE: Delivering Services to Young People in Bristol' in Melrose, M. and Barrett, D. (eds) *Anchors in Floating Lives: Interventions With Young People Sexually Abused Through Prostitution*. Lyme Regis, Dorset: Russell House Publishing (103–14).

Fox, N.J. (2012) *The Body*. Cambridge: Polity Press.

Fuller, A. and Unwin, L. (2011) Vocational education in the spotlight: back to the future for the UK's Coalition government? *London Review of Education*. 9, (2), 191–204.

Furlong, A. and Cartmel, F. (1997) *Young People and Social Change: Individualization and Risk in Late Modernity*. Buckingham: Open University Press.

Gillespie, A. (2005) 'Prostitution or abuse? The Sexual Offences Act 2003'. *Criminal Law Review*. 285–89.

Gillespie, A. (2007) 'Diverting children involved in prostitution'. *Web Journal of Current Legal Issues*. (2).

Goddard, C., De Bortoli, L., Saunders, J. and Tucci, J. (2005) 'The rapists camouflage: "Child Prostitution"'. *Child Abuse Review*. 14, (4), 275–91.

Gorham, D. (1978) '"The Maiden Tribute of Modern Babylon" re-examined. Child prostitution and the idea of childhood in late-Victorian England'. *Victorian Studies*. 21, 353–79.

Green, J. (1992) *It's No Game*. London: National Youth Agency.

Green, J.K., Mulroy, S. and O'Neill, M. (1997) 'Young People and Prostitution from a Youth Service Perspective' in Barrett, D. (eds) *Child Prostitution in Britain*. London: The Children's Society (90–105).

Hallett, S. (2015) "An uncomfortable comfortableness': 'care', child protection and child sexual exploitation'. *British Journal of Social Work*. 10.1093/bjsw/bcv136

Hall, S. and Jefferson, T. (eds) (1993) *Resistance Through Rituals: Youth Subcultures in Post-War Britain*. Abingdon, Oxon: Routledge.

Hall, T. and Coffey, A. (2007) 'Learning selves and citizenship: gender and youth transitions'. *Journal of Social Policy*. 36, (2), 1–18.

Hall, T. and Montgomery, H. (2000) 'Home and away: 'childhood', 'youth' and young people'. *Anthropology Today*. 16, (3), 13–15.

Hayes, C. and Trafford, I. (1997) 'Issues for Voluntary Sector Detached Work Agencies' in Barrett, D. (eds) *Child Prostitution in Britain*. London: The Children's Society (59–75).

House of Commons Home Affairs Committee (HCHAC) (2013) *Child Sexual Exploitation and the Response To Localised Grooming*. London, House of Commons: The Stationery Office.

Hebdige, D. (1979) *Subculture: The Meaning of Style*. London: Routledge.

Hebdige, D. (1988) *Hiding in The Light*. London: Routledge.

Heinze, E. (2000) 'The Universal Child?' in Heinze, E. (ed) *Of Innocence and Autonomy: Children, Sex and Human Rights*. London: Dartmouth Publishing Company (3–25).

Hendrick, H. (2003) *Child Welfare: Historical Dimensions, Contemporary Debate*. Bristol: The Policy Press.

Hendrick, H. (2006) 'Constructions and Reconstructions of British Childhood: An Interpretive Survey, 1800 to the Present' in James, A. and Prout, A. (eds) *Constructing and Reconstructing Childhood* (2nd edition). Abingdon, Oxon: Routledge (34–62).

Hester, M. and Westmarland, N. (2004) *Tackling Street Prostitution: Towards an Holistic Approach*. London: Home Office.

Hickle, K. and Hallett, S. (2016) 'Mitigating harm: considering harm reduction principles in work with sexually exploited young people.' *Children & Society*. 30, (4), 302–13.

Hickson, K. (2010) 'Thatcherism, poverty and social justice'. *Journal of Poverty and Social Justice*. 18, (2), 135–45.

Holland, S. (2010) 'Looked after children and the ethic of care'. *British Journal of Social Work*. 40, 1664–80.

Honneth, A. (2014) *The I in We: Studies in the Theory of Recognition*. Cambridge: Polity Press.

Jago, S., Arocha, L., Brodie, I., Melrose, M., Pearce, J.J. and Warrington, C. (2011) *What's Going On to Safeguard Children and Young People from Sexual Exploitation? How Local Partnerships Respond to Child Sexual Exploitation*. Luton: University of Bedfordshire.

James, A. (2000) 'Embodied Being(s): Understanding the Self and the Body in Childhood' in Prout, A. (ed) *The Body, Childhood and Society*. Hampshire: Macmillan Press (19–37).

James, A. (2009) 'Agency' in Qvortrup J., Corsaro, W.A. and Honig, M.S. (eds) *The Palgrave Handbook of Childhood Studies*. London: Palgrave Macmillan.

James, A. and James, A.L. (2004) *Constructing Childhood: Theory, Policy and Practice*. Hampshire: Palgrave Macmillan.

Jay, A. (2014) *Independent Inquiry into Child. Sexual Exploitation in Rotherham 1997–2013*. Rotherham Council.

Jeffreys, S. (1997) *The Idea of Prostitution*. Australia: Spinnifex Press.

Jeffreys, S. (2000) 'Challenging the child/adult distinction in theory and practice on prostitution'. *International Feminist Journal of Politics.* 2, (3), 359–79.

Jenkins, R. (2004) *Social Identity* (2nd edition). London: Routledge.

Jenks, C. (2000) 'Zeitgeist Research on Childhood' in Christensen, P. and James, A. (eds) *Research with Children*. London: Palmer Press (62–71).

Jesson, J. (1993) 'Understanding adolescent female prostitution: A literature review'. *British Journal of Social Work.* 23, 517–30.

Jordan, B. (2004) 'Emancipatory social work? Opportunity or oxymoron'. *British Journal of Social Work.* 34, (1), 5–19.

Kehily, M.J. and Montgomery, H. (2004) 'Innocence and Experience: a Historical Approach to Childhood and Sexuality' in Kehily, M.J. (ed) *An Introduction to Childhood Studies*. Buckingham: Open University Press (57–74).

Kellett, M., Robinson, C. and Burr, R. (2004) 'Images of Childhood' in Fraser, S., Lewis, V., Ding, S., Kellett, M. and Robinson, C. (eds) *Doing Research With Children and Young People*. London: Sage (27–42).

Kelly, L., Wingfield, R., Burton, S. and Regan, L. (1995) *Splintered Lives: Sexual Exploitation of Children in the Context of Children's Rights and Child Protection*. Barkingside: Barnardo's.

Kerrigan-Lebloch, E. and King, S. (2006) 'Child sexual exploitation: a partnership response and model intervention'. *Child Abuse Review.* 15, (5), 362–72.

Kirby, P. (1995) *A Word from the Street; Young People Who Leave Care and Become Homeless*. London: Centrepoint.

Kitzinger, J. (2006) 'Who are you kidding? Children, Power and the Struggle Against Sexual Abuse' in James, A. and Prout, A. (eds) *Constructing and Reconstructing Childhood* (2nd edition). Abingdon, Oxon: Routledge (165–89).

La Fontaine, J. (1998) *Speak of The Devil: Tales of Satanic Abuse in Contemporary England*. Cambridge: Cambridge University Press.

Lee, N. (2001) *Childhood and Society: Growing Up in an Age of Uncertainty*. Buckingham: Open University Press.

Leeson, C. (2007) 'My life in care: experiences of non-participation in decision-making processes'. *Child and Family Social Work.* 12, 268–77.

Lillywhite, R. and Skidmore, P. (2006) 'Boys are not sexually exploited? A challenge to practitioners'. *Child Abuse Review.* 15, (5), 351–61.

Lowe, K. and Pearce, J.J. (2006) 'Young people and prostitution'. *Child Abuse Review.* 15, (5), 289–93.

Marshall, H. and Stenner, P. (2004) 'Friends and Lovers' in Roche, J., Tucker, S., Thomson, R. and Flyn, R. (eds) *Youth in Society: Contemporary Theory, Policy and Practice*. London: Sage (184–90).

McMullen, R. (1987) 'Youth prostitution: a balance of power'. *Journal of Adolescence.* 10, 35–43.

McRobbie, A. (1991) *Feminism and Youth Culture: From "Jackie" to "Just Seventeen".* New York: Routledge.

Melrose, M. (2004) 'Of Tricks and Other Things: An Overview' in Melrose, M. with Barrett, D. (eds) *Anchors in Floating Lives: Interventions with Young People Sexually Abused Through Prostitution.* Lyme Regis, Dorset: Russell House Publishing (1–12).

Melrose, M. (2010) 'What's love got to do with it? Theorising young people's involvement in prostitution'. *Youth and Policy.* 104, 12–31.

Melrose, M. (2012) 'Twenty-first century party people: young people and sexual exploitation in the new millennium'. *Child Abuse Review.* 22, (3), 155–68.

Melrose, M., Barrett, D. and Brodie, I. (1999) *One Way Street? Retrospectives on Childhood Prostitution.* London: The Children's Society.

Melrose, M. and Pearce, J. (eds) (2013) *Critical Perspectives on Child Sexual Exploitation and Related Trafficking.* Hampshire: Palgrave Macmillan.

Montgomery, H. (1998) 'Children, Prostitution and dentity' in Kempadoo, K. and Doezema, J. (eds) *Global Sex Workers: Rights, Resistance, and Redefinition.* London: Routledge (139–50).

Montgomery, H. (2009) *An Introduction to Childhood: Anthropological Perspectives on Children's Lives.* Sussex: Wiley Blackwell.

Moore, M. (2006) 'Should young people involved in the sex industry be seen as victims?'. *The Police Journal.* 79, (1), 77–89.

Morrow, V., and Richards, M. (1996) *Transitions to Adulthood: A Family Matter?* York: Joseph Rowntree Foundation.

Newman, C. (1989) *Young Runaways: Findings from Britain's First Safe House.* London: The Children's Society.

NSPCC (2003) *The Choice and Opportunities Project.* Middlesex: NSPCC.

Nussbaum, M. (1998) '"Whether from Reason or Prejudice" Making Money for Bodily Services' in Spector, J. (ed) (2006) *Prostitution and Pornography: Philosophical Debate about the Sex Industry.* Stanford, California: Stanford University Press (175–208).

O'Connell Davidson, J. (2005) *Children in the Global Sex Trade.* Cambridge: Polity Press.

O'Connell Davidson, J. (2011) 'Moving children? Child trafficking, child migration, and child rights'. *Critical Social Policy.* 31, (3), 454–77.

O'Connell Davidson, J. and Anderson, B. (2006) 'The Trouble with 'Trafficking'' in Van den Anker, C.L. and Doomernick, J. (eds) *Trafficking and Women's Rights.* Hampshire: Palgrave (11–26).

Ofsted (2014) *The sexual exploitation of children: it couldn't happen here, could it?'* Ofsted thematic report. https://www.gov.uk/government/publications/sexual-exploitation-of-children-ofsted-thematic-report

O'Neill, M. (2001) *Prostitution and Feminism: Towards a Politics of Freedom.* Cambridge: Polity Press.

O'Neill, M., Goode, N. and Hopkins, K. (1995) 'Juvenile prostitution: the experience of young women in residential care'. *Childright*. 113, 14–16.

Palmer, T. (2001) *No Son of Mine! Children Abused through Prostitution*. Barkingside: Barnardo's.

Paskell, C. (2012) *Tackling Child Sexual Exploitation: Helping Local Authorities to Develop Effective Responses*. Barkingside; Barnardo's.

Pateman, C. (2006) 'What's Wrong With Prostitution' in Spector, J. (ed) (2006) *Prostitution and Pornography: Philosophical Debate about the Sex Industry*. Stanford, California: Stanford University Press (50–79).

Pearce, J.J. (2006) 'Finding the 'I' in Sexual Exploitation: Young People's Voices Within Policy and Practice' in Cambell, R. and O'Neill, M.(eds) *Sex Work Now*. Devon: Willan Publishing (190–211).

Pearce, J.J. (2007) 'Risk and Resilience: A Focus on Sexually Exploited Young People' in Thom, B., Sales, R. and Pearce. J.J (eds) *Growing up with Risk*. University of Bristol: The Policy Press (203–18).

Pearce, J.J. (2009) *Young People and Sexual Exploitation: It's Not Hidden, You Just Aren't Looking*. Abingdon, Oxon: Routledge.

Pearce, J.J. (2010) 'Young People, sexual exploitation and trafficking: C contemporary issues in connecting discourses of child abuse and child protection'. *Youth and Policy*. 104, 32–46.

Pearce, J.J. (2013) 'A Social Model of "Abused Consent"' in Melrose, M. and Pearce, J.J (eds) *Critical Perspectives on Child Sexual Exploitation and Related Trafficking*. London: Palgrave Macmillan (52–68).

Pearce, J.J. with Williams, M. and Galvin, C. (2002) *It's Someone Taking a Part of You: A Study of Young Women and Sexual Exploitation*. London: National Children's Bureau.

Pearson, G. (1983) *Hooligan: A History of Respectable Fears*. London: Macmillan.

Phoenix, J. (2002) 'In the name of protection: youth prostitution reforms in England and Wales'. *Critical Social Policy*. 22, (2), 353–75.

Phoenix, J. (2010) 'Living on the cusp of contradictions: consumerism, justice and closed discourses'. *Youth and Policy*. 104, 32–46.

Phoenix, J., and Oerton, S. (2005). *Illicit and Illegal: Sex, Regulation and Social Control*. Collumpton, Devon: Willan Publishing.

Piper, C. (2000) 'Historical Constructions of Childhood Innocence: Removing Sexuality' in Heinze, E. (ed) *Of Innocence and Autonomy: Children, Sex and Human Rights*. Aldershot: Dartmouth Publishing Company (26–45).

Pithouse, A. (2008) 'Early intervention in the round: a great idea but...'. *British Journal of Social Work*. 38, 1536–52.

Pithouse, A., Broadhurst, K., Hall, C., Peckover, S., Wastell, D. and White, S. (2011) 'Trust, risk and the (mis)management of contingency and discretion through new information technologies in Children's Services'. *Journal of Social Work*. 12, (2), 158–78.

Pitts, J. (1997) 'Causes of Youth Prostitution, New Forms of Practice and Political Responses' in Barrett, D. (ed) *Child Prostitution in Britain*. London: The Children's Society (139–57).

Prout, A. (2000) 'Childhood Bodies: Construction, Agency and Hybridity' in Prout, A. (ed) *The Body, Childhood and Society*. Hampshire: Macmillan Press (1–18).

Prout, A., and James, A. (2006) 'A New Paradigm for the Sociology of Childhood? Provenance, Promise and Problems' in James, A. and Prout, A. (eds) *Constructing and Reconstructing Childhood* (2nd edition). Abingdon, Oxon: Routledge (7–33).

Punch, S. (2005) *Introduction to Social Research: Qualitative and Quantitative Approach* (2nd edition). London: Sage.

Rees, A. and Pithouse, A. (2008) 'The intimate world of strangers – embodying the child in foster care'. *Child and Family Social Work*. 13, 338–47.

Renold, E. (2007) Primary school 'studs': (de)constructing young boys' heterosexual masculinities'. *Men and Masculinities*. 9, (3), 275–98.

Saunders, P. (2005) 'Identity to Acronym: How "child prostitution" became "CSEC"' in Bernstein, E. and Schaffner, L. (eds) *Regulating Sex: the Politics of intimacy and identity*. New York: Routledge (167–88).

Scott, S. and Skidmore, P. (2006) *Reducing the Risk: Barnardo's Support for Sexually Exploited Young People: A Two Year Evaluation*. Barkingside: Barnardo's.

Seng, M. (1989) 'Child sexual abuse and adolescent prostitution: a comparative analysis'. *Adolescence*. 24, (95), 665–75.

Sennett, R. (2003) *Respect*. London: Penguin.

Shaw, I., Butler, I., Crowley, A. and Patel, G. (1996) *Paying the Price: Young People and Prostitution in South Glamorgan*. Cardiff: Cardiff University, School of Social and Administrative Studies.

Shaw, I., and Butler, I. (1998) 'Understanding young people and prostitution: a foundation for practice?'. *British Journal of Social Work*. 28, 177–96.

Shuker, L. (2013) 'Constructs of Safety for Children in Care Affected by Sexual Exploitation' in Melrose, M. and Pearce, J.J (eds) *Critical Perspectives on Child Sexual Exploitation and Related Trafficking*. Hampshire: Palgrave Macmillan (125–38).

Smith, C., Stainton-Rogers, W. and Tucker, S. (2007) 'Risk' in Robb, M. (ed) *Youth in Context: Frameworks, Settings and Encounters*. London: Sage (219–50).

Spector, J. (ed) (2006) *Prostitution and Pornography: Philosophical Debate about the Sex Industry*. Stanford, California: Stanford University Press.

Sturrock, R. and Holmes, L. (2015) *Running the Risks: The links between gang involvement and young people going missing*. London: Catch 22.

Swann, S., and Balding, V. (2001) *Guidance Review: Safeguarding Children Involved in Prostitution*. London: Department of Health.

Taylor-Browne, J. (2002) *More Than One Chance: Young People Involved in Prostitution Speak Out*. London: ECPAT UK.

UNICEF (2001) *Profiting from Abuse: The Sexual Exploitation of Our Children*. New York: UNICEF.

Valentine, G. (2004) *Public Space and the Culture of Childhood*. Aldershot: Ashgate Publishing.

Van Meeuwen, A., Swann, S., McNeish, D. and Edwards, S. (1998) *Whose Daughter Next? Children abused through prostitution*. Barkingside, Essex: Barnardo's.

WAG (2011) *Safeguarding Children and Young People from Sexual Exploitation. Supplementary guidance to Safeguarding Children: Working Together Under the Children Act 2004*. Cardiff: WAG.

Warrington, C. (2010) 'From less harm to more good: the role of children and young people's participation in relation to sexual exploitation'. *Youth and Policy*. 104, 62–79.

Wastell, D., White, S., Broadhurst, K., Peckover, S. and Pithouse, A. (2010) 'Children's services in the iron cage of performance management: street-level bureaucracy and the spectre of Švejkism'. *International Journal of Social Welfare*. 19, (3), 310–20.

Weisburg, D.K. (1985) *Children of the Night: A Study of Adolescent Prostitution*. Lexington, Massachusetts: Lexington Books.

Williams, L.M. (2010) 'Harm and resilience among prostituted teens: broadening our understanding of victimisation and survival'. *Social Policy and Society*. 9, (2), 243–54.

Williams, S. (1999) *The Commercial Sexual Exploitation of Children in Jamaica*. Kingston: Caribbean Child Development Centre.

Willis, P. (1977) *Learning to Labour*. Aldershot: Gower.

Willis, P. (1990) *Common Culture: Symbolic Work at Play in The Everyday Culture of The Young*. Buckingham: Open University Press.

Winter, K. (2010) 'The perspectives of young children in care about their circumstances and implications for social work practice'. *Child & Family Social Work*. 15, (2), 186–95.

Wulff, H. and Amit, V.T. (eds) (1995) *Youth Cultures: A Cross-cultural Perspective*. London: Routledge.

Wyn, J. and White, R. (1997) *Rethinking Youth*. London: Sage.

YWCA (2002) 'Not a game: young women and prostitution'. *YWCA Briefing*. 5, 1–8.

Index

A

abduction 13
absconding 16, 38, 48
abusers 25, 85, 122
  adult 68, 72
  and family 87
accommodation 16, 21, 22, 29, 95, 99
  see also secure accommodation
acknowledgement 86, 90, 115
Adams, N. 19
adolescence 30–1
advocacy 130
agency 11, 28, 31, 91, 101, 133
  and choice 146–9
  ignoring 21
  lack of 18
  and risk 70–5
  sense of 67
  understanding 78–82
  and victim status 142
alcohol 18, 55, 58–60, 69, 81, 84, 92, 109
Alexander, C. and Charles, G. 120
Asian men 8
Association of Moral and Social Hygiene (AMSH) 13
Ayre, P. and Barrett, D. 27

B

Barnardo's 23
behaviour 22, 59, 62
believed, being 118
benefits 16
Berger, J. 140
blame 13, 18, 81
body, ownership of 43, 52, 61, 81, 92, 108
boundaries
  confused 108
  definition of 102–3
  professional 134
  sexual 42–5, 65–6, 120
  and structure 125–7
Boyden, J. 26
boyfriends 17
boys, as offenders 77
brainwashing 84–7, 151
Brown, A. 27
Brown, A. and Barrett, D. 13–14
bullying 16, 93–5

C

care 4–5, 16, 22, 36–9, 64
  acts of 128
  changes in 42
  failures of 49–50
  foster 107, 125
  lack of 111
  longer term 130, 141
  a negative experience 149
  relationships 44–5
  response 21
Casey, L. 78–9
Centre for Contemporary Social Studies (CCCS) 30
Chicago School of social ecology 30
child sexual exploitation
  definition 23, 83–4, 144
  overview 11–32
  responding to 124–7, 139–42
Child Sexual Exploitation in Gangs and Groups 83
childhood 27–9
childlikeness 77–8
Children Act 1989 15
Children's Commissioner for England 83
choices 17, 73, 146–9
coercion 17, 24, 144 *see also* manipulation
  and grooming 84–8
  and manipulation 91, 94, 98
Cohen, Stanley 29–30
Coles, J. 22
Colwell, Maria 14
complexity 80, 152–3
confidentiality 121
consent 17, 85, 93, 95, 97, 101
  and agency 146–53
  assumptions about 78
  inability to 24, 26, 68, 80, 105
  interpretation of 74–5
  matters of 107
coping behaviours 55, 84, 109, 139
  and exchanging sex 96–9
  and risk 58–63
counselling *see* talking
Coy, M. 22
criminal 11, 12, 16, 83
Cusick, L. 24